Defending in Soccer

For Professors David Owen Kieft and John Kim Munholland

TONY ENGLUND

DEFENDING IN SOCCER

THE COMPREHENSIVE GUIDE

Meyer & Meyer Sport

British Library of Cataloguing in Publication Data
A catalogue record for this book is available from the British Library

Defending in Soccer
Maidenhead: Meyer & Meyer Sport (UK) Ltd., 2024
ISBN: 978-1-78255-235-2

© 2024 by Meyer & Meyer Sport (UK) Ltd.
Aachen, Auckland, Beirut, Cairo, Cape Town, Dubai, Hägendorf, Hong Kong, Indianapolis, Maidenhead, Manila, New Delhi, Singapore, Sydney, Tehran, Vienna

Member of the World Sport Publishers' Association (WSPA), www.w-s-p-a.org

Printed by Versa Press, East Peoria, IL
Printed in the United States of America

ISBN: 978-1-78255-235-2
Email: info@m-m-sports.com
www.thesportspublisher.com

The content of this book was carefully researched. All information is supplied without liability. Neither the author nor the publisher will be liable for possible disadvantages, injuries, or damages.

CONTENTS

Acknowledgments...11
Introduction 14

Technical Defending 17
   Defending Footwork:
      Line Exercise..18
      Jockey Zig-Zag (1)...19
      Jockey Zig-Zag (2)...20
      Jockey Zig-Zag (3)...21
      Line Jockey 22
      Line Jockey and Tackle...23
      Cones..24
      Priorities (1)–Deny Ball...25
      Priorities (2a)–Deny Turn..26
      Priorities (2b)–Deny Turn..27
      Priorities (3a)–Deny Penetration 28
      Priorities (3b)–Deny Penetration 29
      Priorities (4)–Deny Shot...30
      Separating Opponent From the Ball.................................31
      Separating Opponent From the Ball in a Live Exercise...........32
      Close Down and Recover 34
      Block Tackle 35
      Poke Tackle (1) 37
      Poke Tackle (2) 38
      Slide Tackle 40
      1v1: Knock Out 42
      Knee Tag...43
      Ball Tag 45
      Close Down and Control in a Grid...................................46
   Dueling: Winning 1v1 Duels...47
      1v1 Continuous 47
      1v1 "Kill Touch" 49
      1v1 "Swimming" to Win the Duel 50
      1v1 Immediate Pressure 52
      1v1 Immediate Pressure With Server................................54
      1v1 to a Side Cone Goal...55

1v1 to Two Side Cone Goals...56
1v1 Call Start...57
1v1 Throw-In...58
1v1 Long Grid With Long Pass..60
1v1 Chip..62
1v1 Juggle and Volley...63
1v1 Back-to-Back...64
1v1 to a Center Cone/Ball Goal...65
1v1 2 Cone Ball Goals..66
1v1 to a Central Stick Goal...67
1v1 50/50 Ball...68
1v1 to Small Goals: Speed..69
1v1 Defender Chase...70
1v1 Recovery Duels...71
1v1 Two Grids..72
1v1 Four Goals..73
1v1 to Goal...74
1v1 Continuous to Goal...75
1v1 Box Duels..77
1v1 Defending "Flat" Near the Goal..78
1v1 Bogie Alley...80
1v1 Corner Duels..81
1v1 Ladder..82
1v1 Deny Pass...84
1v1 Deny Cross...86
1v1 Defend Crosses Near Goal..89
1v1 Attacker Facing Away (1)..91
1v1 Attacker Facing Away (2)..92
1v1 Attacker Facing Away (3)..94
1v1 Attacker Facing Away (4)..95
1v1 Long Gride With Long Pass Service...96
1v1 Air Duels: Side-by-Side...97
1v1 Aerial Duels Front and Back (1)..99
Aerial Duels Front and Back (2)...100
Aerial Defending: Serves, Throw-Ins, Punts...............................102
1v1 Defend Throw-In (1)..104
1v1 Defend Throw-In (2)..106
Defending Footwork: Recognize 1v2...107
1v2 Bumper (1)..109

1v2 Bumper (2)..110
1V2 Bumper (3)..112
1v Unknown..113
Second Defenders: Cover and Double 114
Second Defender (1):
Movement and Communication (1)..115
Movement and Communication (2)..117
Team Warm-Up (1) 118
Team Warm-Up (2) 119
Double-Team (1)..120
Double-Team (2)..121
2v2 in a Grid (1)..123
2v2 in a Gride (2)..124
2v2 in a Grid—Preventing 1–2 Combinations (A)............................125
2v2 in a Grid—Preventing 1–2 Combinations (B)............................126
Emphasis 4v2 Rondo (1) 127
Emphasis 4v2 Rondo (2) 128
Emphasis 4v2 Rondo (3) 129
Emphasis 4v2 Rondo: High Pressure 130
2v2+4:
Second Defender Emphasis 131
Second Defender Interchange 133
Second Defender Screening Through Pass 134
Second Defender Preventing Combinations by Attackers................135
Second Defender (2):
1v2 18-Yard Box (1)..137
1v2 18-Yard Box (2)..139
1v2 18-Yard Box, Attacker Facing Away..140
Emphasis: 2v2 18-Yard Box..141
Emphasis: 2v2 18-Yard Box—Alternative Defending
Approach...142
Deny Cross (1) 143
Deny Cross (2) 145
Double-Team (1)..146
Double-Team (2)..148
Double-Team (3)..149
4v4 Game to Double-Team 151
5v4 to Corner Goals—Double-Team Emphasis................................153
4v4 in the Area—Double-Team Emphasis 155

Third Defenders: Group Balance...157
    Third Defender:
        8v8 Four-Zone Game (1)...158
        8v8 Four-Zone Game (2)...159
        8v8 Four-Zone Game (3)...160
        8v8 Four-Zone Game (4)...161
        Zone Game (1)...162
        Zone Game (2)...163
        Zone Game (3)...164
        Zone Game (4)...165
Defending From the Front: Tactical Considerations for
Front-Line Players...167
    Forward Defending:
        Center Forward (1)...168
        Center Forward (2)...169
        Center Forward (3)...170
        Wingers (1)..173
        Wingers (2)..175
        Two Strikers Defending Wide (1)..176
        Two Strikers Defending Wide (2)..177
        Two Strikers Defending Wide (3)..178
        Two Strikers Defending Centrally (1)..180
        Single-Striker Systems (1)..182
        Single-Striker Systems (2)..183
Defending From the Midfield: The Importance of
Mobility and Flexibility...185
    Defending in the Midfield:
        Standard Three-Person Midfield (1)...187
        Standard Three-Person Midfield (2)—Areas of Concern...................................188
        Standard Three-Person Midfield (3)—Principal Actions....................................190
        Standard Three-Person Midfield (4)—Against Withdrawn
        Midfielder..191
        Standard Three-Person Midfield (5)—Against Wide
        Penetration by Midfielder...193
        Flipped Triangle General Considerations...194
        Four Players, Flat Configuration: Areas of Concern..196
        Four Players, Flat Configuration: Ball Out Wide..198
        Four Players, Flat Configuration: Ball Central..200
        Four Players, Diamond Configuration: Areas of Concern...................................201

Four Players, Box Configuration: Areas of Concern 203
Five Players: Areas of Concern 204
Defending Along the Back Line: Consistency and Coordination........................ 206
Modern Back Four in Possession and
Transition: Space and Time 207
Back Four in Defensive Transition Against Faced-Up
Attackers in the Middle Third: Drop and Close Seams............................. 209
Back Four in Defensive Transition: When Should a Player Step
Forward to Challenge?.. 210
Back Four Defending:
    Common Mistakes by Young Defenders... 212
    Dealing With Wide Spaces in the Back Third 214
Back-Line Defending: Three Center Backs... 216
The Goalkeeper's Role in Team Defending 218
Back-Pass to Goalkeeper in Support of Back Line 219
Goalkeeper Clearance on Ball Behind Back Line.................................... 220
Goalkeeper and Defender Dealing With Potential
Break-Away 222
Goalkeeper and Back-Line Defending Crosses...................................... 224
Tactical Group Defending: Pressing and Counter-Pressing 226
Individual Pressing.. 227
Pairs Pressing (1)... 228
Pairs Pressing (2)... 229
4v4 Pressing to Four Goals 230
4v5 + Goalkeeper Pressing 231
Spine for Team A 236
Team A Press Design Basics... 238
Team A Press Basics:
    Where to Funnel the Ball... 240
    Forcing the Ball to the Touchline.. 241
    "Safety" Player.. 242
    Trigger 1 243
    Trigger 2 245
    Trigger 3 246
1v1 Counter-Press.. 248
3v3 Counter-Press.. 249
5v5 Counter-Press to End-Line Targets 250
8v8 Counter-Pressing Game 252
11v11 Counter-Pressing Training Match 254

Tactical Group Defending: Delayed High Pressure...256
    11v11 Delayed High Pressure..257
    Team Defending From a Mid Block...259
    Defending From a Low Block..260
Stronghold Defending—A Tactical Revolution...262
    Standard Team Shape: Defending Kick-Offs...271
    Defending Kick-Offs: High Pressure...272
    Defending Goal Kicks: A Standard Look 273
    Defending Goal Kicks: Tempting the Opponent to Play
    Short 274
    Defending Punts: Concentration and Depth 275
    Defending Corner Kicks:
        "Man" Marking...276
        Zonal Schemes...278
        Zone/Person-Marking Mix 280
        Dealing With Short Plays by the Opponent.....................................282
        Dealing With a Player Screening the Goalkeeper 284
    Defending Free Kicks:
        Free Kick From Distance..286
        Slowing the Kick and Setting the Defense (1)................................288
        Slowing the Kick and Setting the Defense (2)................................290
        Setting the Defense (3)..292
        A Taller Wall? (4)..293
        Adding a "Bullet" (5)...294
Defending Set Pieces: Efficient, Lively Training..296
    Down a Player...297
    Playing With a Lead (1)...298
    Playing With a Lead (2)...298
    Playing From Behind 299
    Down a Goal 299

Conclusion..302
Bibliography and Suggested Reading 303

ACKNOWLEDGMENTS

American First Lady Eleanor Roosevelt is credited with uttering the phrase, "Do one thing every day that scares you." That's exactly what this project did for me for the entire research and writing period. As a coach, I'm among the guilty who have undertreated the subject of defending in the teams I coach. Without exception, I'd rather coach finishing than low-block defending. I find attacking patterns much more intriguing than how to defend crosses in detail. For most of us, though not all, this is part of the culture of our game. The attacking is the exciting, plannable portion of the game, and the defending is only necessary to get the ball back.

For those reasons, as well as the more global feel that the attacking wizards have run the show in soccer coaching for decades now, it was time to point out that we're neglecting defending in our game and that a comprehensive response to the attacking innovation is the next logical philosophical step in the thinking about soccer.

This was, indeed, a scary proposition. How do we begin to rectify the imbalance in our coaching between the attack and defense, and from where do we cull the best in defensive coaching? For those answers, in particular, I owe debts of gratitude to mentors, colleagues, and family.

Many thanks, as always, to Liz Evans and Martin Meyer of Meyer & Meyer publishing. Liz, in particular, has been, without fail, patient, supportive, and full of good ideas and guidance throughout the publishing process, and I am indebted to her for her support.

When I first proposed this project and was mulling the implications and directions of the research, Mark Backlund sent me a message that crystallized much of my thinking about why this topic was timely. Mark and I played indoor soccer together 20 and more years ago, and he was a prototypical defender: poised, timely, and crisp in his defending and distribution out of the back. His support, again, confirmed much of my thinking.

Conversations with colleagues, as well as observation of their work on the field, often lead to improvement and expansion of my own thinking, and a number of coaching friends have contributed to varying degrees to my understanding of defending. Nathan Klonecki, Mike Huber, Jake Smothers, Matt Carlson, Joaquin Izquierdo, Phil Walczak, Amanda Maxwell, Marcos Rodriguez, Tim Magnuson, and many other coaches at St. Croix Soccer Club do outstanding work with their young players every day, which has helped frame my understanding of defending. Mark Yueill, a coach and director for the Minnesota Thunder Academy, is an incredible student of the game, whose grasp of the subtleties of coaching and high standards are evident in the play of his teams and also the success of his son, Jackson and his daughter, Maddy.

The late Dick Bate was, without a doubt, the most thoughtful clinician of our game. I have often stated that I could not write fast enough when he talked. I met him in 2011 and, after that, raced to anywhere in the country where he was scheduled to present. Always kind and patient, he spent time with many of us, talking about the nuances of the game and the best ways to teach our players. Through the efforts of his wife and coaching friends, the *Dick Bate Football Anthology* was published online after his passing as a fundraiser for the Giles' Trust, which carries out research to help treat brain tumors. The resulting document contains more than 3,000 pages of Coach Bate's training sessions and writing on a wide range of soccer topics. It is, to me, a teaching course without parallel and a tour de force on defending in particular. Here is the web address for those interested: https://gilestrust.org/blogs/the-dick-bate-football-anthology. I think of Coach Bate every time I go on the field, and his writings and teachings deeply influence my thinking on defensive planning and instruction.

I have been coaching soccer teams for more than 30 years now. Thoughts of the people I have coached are never far from my mind, and I am very thankful for the memories of all the different groups with whom I have worked. I want to recognize the 1998 guys (7th and 6th in the USA), and the 2004 boys (NPL Final Four) in particular.

Professors David Owen Kieft and John Kim Munholland, to whom this book is jointly dedicated, were advisors to my MA thesis on military history. Two charismatic, brilliant role models who showed considerable patience with me. I think of them often and miss talking with them both.

Two mentors in particular have been kind enough to support my coaching and writing efforts. Jeff Tipping, Director of Coaching Education Emeritus for the NSCAA (now USC), has been a consistent source of encouragement for many years, and our occasional conversations about coaching and the world, in general, are invariably heartening. John Pascarella, former head coach at Oklahoma City Energy (USL 1), is one of my favorite people because of his sharp sense of humor and never-ending curiosity and optimism about coaching. We have co-authored two books and any time talking with him is memorable and energizing for me. He read the manuscript for this book and suggested several important changes.

I also want to thank my parents, Tony and Carole Englund, and my wife, Beth, for their support of my coaching and writing over the years.

INTRODUCTION: STRONGHOLD DEFENDING—AN IN-DEPTH FORMULA FOR WINNING THE BALL

"Defending is just effort," according to many, many soccer coaches at all levels and for decades. It's tantalizing to think about the balance, or lack thereof, in how the game of soccer is coached between the attacking side and the defending side. Coaching literature, clinics, licensing courses, websites, and YouTube all feature an impressive array of compelling information on subjects ranging from ball striking and moves to beat opponents to sneaky set pieces and all manner of goals. To be sure, there are occasional highlight reels of risky but successful slide tackles and eye-popping goalkeeper saves, and the vogue topic of pressing has been the subject of much analysis in recent years. Still, the attention given to defending topics pales in comparison with that given to attacking.

Pep Guardiola, of FC Barcelona, Bayern Munich and Manchester City coaching fame, and a defensive midfielder in his playing days, is, for me, symbolic of how even the world's elite coaches tend to obsess with the details of attacking philosophy at the expense of developing an evolving, detailed defending culture. Guardiola famously expected his players at Barcelona to win the ball back within 6 seconds and is credited with having said, "We're terrible without the ball. We must have the ball." This desperate approach is a useful motivator (and foreshadowed the coming emphasis on pressing), but the fragility of Guardiola's teams on the defensive side of the ball in the biggest matches is arguably indicative of the disdain that their head coach felt regarding the importance of a comprehensive defending scheme.

That said, who among us could say that we devote as much energy, thought, and training time to defending topics as we do to the attacking side of the ball? This conundrum is especially disconcerting in light of the fact that most teams spend nearly half of any given match without the ball. To be sure, defending topics for most of us are not as much fun to teach, and the players typically share their coaches' lack of enthusiasm for lengthy, detailed discussions of how to behave without the ball. Furthermore, this distaste for defending topics has a cumulative effect as the lack of interest and demand for organized planning on the defensive side of the ball is compounded with each succeeding generation of coaches and teams.

The past 30 years have witnessed a series of rules changes, tactical innovations, and rapid evolution improving the attacking side of the game. The back-pass rule change, which prevented goalkeepers from using their hands when receiving a ball played to them from their teammates, became a bookend to an era in the 1980s that featured a lot of layered, physical defending and endless tactical delays by teams wanting to slow or kill the game. Subsequently, the emphasis on technical improvement, attacking design, and throwing increasing numbers forward, as well as more stringent regulation of physical play, have produced an era of flowing, entertaining soccer.

Arguably the most recent revolution in soccer has been the heavy focus on transition moments. Pressing and counterattacking, most notably on display in Jürgen Klopp's spectacularly successful Liverpool side but in evidence now across the soccer world, might seem to indicate the value of defending, but much pressing (not that practiced at Liverpool!) is, one could argue, an effort to actually avoid developing a detailed defending philosophy. Indeed, this appears to be the Achilles' heel of the aforementioned Guardiola teams. While the many shades of pressing have been shown to offer an effective first line of defense, much less detailed thought and planning has been put forth by many teams regarding what to do when their pressing does not result in recovery of possession.

This book is an effort to encapsulate all of the best defending practices in modern soccer. From basic defending technique, which is something of a lost art, to complex, layered tactical planning at team level, there is much thought-provoking material here for coaches at any level. There is a blend of instructional photos, diagrams, and exemplary press pictures of the world's best players included in support of the text. The aim is to provide a comprehensive, accessible "idea" book that coaches can consult to help plan their defensive strategy and sessions and also diagnose and correct issues as the team evolves.

This study will also take the further step of advocating *stronghold* defending. Merriam-Webster defines a stronghold as, "A place of security or survival."

Bending this idea to a soccer context, *stronghold defending* will be a reference to building a tiered, comprehensive defending scheme that conditions the team to defend in concert and win the ball anywhere on the field. It's important to note that each team's *stronghold* will look different, depending on the designs of the coach and the abilities and needs of the team. Some teams will emphasize early and heavy pressing, while others will want to put more energy into developing a low block from which to win the ball. However, the overriding message will be that if the team wishes to maximize its ability to defend, it will be necessary to imprint all the concepts introduced in this book and then blend the ideas to create an in-depth, flexible stronghold from which to defend and win the ball.

TECHNICAL DEFENDING

It's cliché to state that the weakest link in any chain limits the strength of that unit when referring to team defending. As simple as the notion is, it's also true. Particularly at the higher levels of the game, teams will scout and identify the opponent's least-able defenders and then try to orient their attacks to expose that player. It is, therefore, critical that, even at the youth levels, coaches work to strengthen individual players' defending abilities as part of improving team-level defending.

Technical defending is a term encompassing all the basic elements required for individual players to defend. *Footwork* and *tackling*, as well as *defensive heading* are the most common elements associated with technical defending. Refining these skills as well as the decision making entailed in using these elements should be a standard ingredient in any defending session.

DEFENDING FOOTWORK: LINE EXERCISE

This is a good exercise to highlight the importance of clean, explosive footwork for defenders involving movement forward and back. Players often need to check their approach to the ball or an opponent based on the development of the situation, and it is often necessary to back off quickly without losing defending posture and balance and then be able to push forward again very quickly.

The active player runs to the first cone and does footwork around the cone before proceeding to the second cone, where she repeats the circle footwork. Then she runs to the tall cone and gets set to defend (set her feet, showing the ball to her left). Next, she backs off to the other tall cone before sprinting to the ball at the top of the setup. Finally, the players jog back along the side of the exercise to the start point. The next player starts when the player in front has reached the first tall cone. Players should alternate the direction of their circular footwork with each new trip through the exercise.

DEFENDING FOOTWORK: JOCKEY ZIG-ZAG (1)

English coaching legend Dick Bate often quoted long-time Italian national team captain Paolo Maldini as stating, "If I had to tackle, I had already made a mistake." The point was that Maldini believed that footwork was the key component to defending. Jockeying, which is using short chop steps, to control an attacker is a skill that has to be taught and refined in all field players and particularly back-line players. Jockeying allows the defender to maintain a focus on the ball and sustain a goal-side orientation to the attacker until the defender finds the right moment to tackle.

This introductory exercise creates a low-pressure environment for players to work on jockeying under the observation of the coach. The defender passes the ball to the attacker and then closes down, running forward to meet the attacker. The attacker waits for the defender to arrive and then begins to dribble through the zig-zag cone pattern. The defender cannot tackle but practices jockeying, focusing on the ball, and using chop steps to stay goal side.

DEFENDING FOOTWORK: JOCKEY ZIG-ZAG (2)

This diagram shows the progression of the exercise. The attacker has made the first turn, and the defender continues to give ground to maintain a goal-side position. Encourage the attacker to change speeds and even directions within the zig-zag, forcing the defender to adjust. When the pair reach the last cone, they switch lines, and the next pair restarts the exercise.

As defending players become more comfortable and cleaner with their footwork, the coach can progress the exercise by allowing the defenders to tackle near the final cone and/or let the attackers freestyle dribble and permit the defenders to tackle.

DEFENDING FOOTWORK: JOCKEY ZIG-ZAG (3)

The final drill in this series highlights the importance of the defender changing her footwork to stay with and ultimately guide the attacker. When the attacker changes direction at the cone, the defender changes her footwork (her lead foot and orientation) to remain open to the attacker's dribble and to be in a good position to tackle. Defenders must become adept at seamlessly changing their footwork to maintain a good position as the attackers become more adept at changing speed and direction, as well as penetrating.

DEFENDING FOOTWORK: LINE JOCKEY

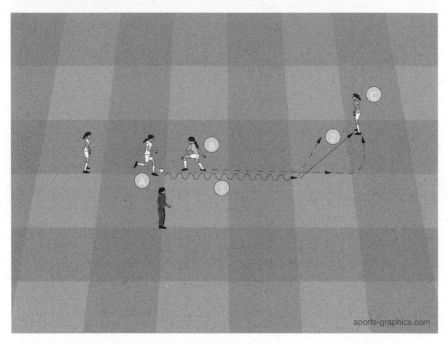

Player A dribbles straight ahead, while player B jockeys, maintaining proper distance and emphasizing clean footwork and focus on the ball. When A nears the far cone, she passes to player C and then moves to jockey player C's dribble back to her own line. No tackling is allowed at this stage. This is a very good warm-up exercise to help players both get some touches on the ball and also do some defending footwork, perhaps in preparation for a 1v1 exercise.

DEFENDING FOOTWORK: LINE JOCKEY AND TACKLE

sports-graphics.com

In this progression of the previous exercise, the defender (B) jockeys and then moves to block tackle the attacker (A). Both players trap the ball between their feet, and then the defender backs off and continues jockeying the attacker's dribble until the latter passes to player C and the exercise continues.

Once again, this is a great warm-up exercise, adding the opportunity to mix in a block tackle for both active players. The fact that the defender must recover after tackling and continue tracking the attacker is an added positive reinforcement.

Another variation here is to have the defender fake tackle. In this instance, player B would jockey and then take a sharp step forward to disrupt the attacker's dribble and planning. The defender must understand that faking the tackle when too close to the attacker can result in the attacker getting in behind, so she has to maintain a bit of extra space and then recover quickly.

DEFENDING FOOTWORK: CONES

Two players practice closing down at cones, moving with cues from the coach. Each player has six cones, in three colors. Emphasize quality movement over speed, but encourage players to move at speed between shut down moments. Check the movements and final positions of the players as they work. Most players will take a few reps to learn to move cleanly, and then they will tire after about 15 seconds of intensive work.

Commands:

- "Red!"—a color call instructs the player to close down the color in the line the defenders face.

- "Turn!"—leads the defender to turn around and shut down the same color in the other line on their end of the area.

- "Switch!"—the players exchange cone work areas (i.e., the player in the bottom cone group moves to the top group and vice versa).

- "Next!"—means that the players sprint out of the grid and the next defender comes in to the area.

DEFENDING FOOTWORK: PRIORITIES (1)— DENY BALL

Defending players should be taught to view every individual defending situation as a set of descending priorities. There are four decisions within this context, and the first preference is to *deny the ball.* If possible, the defender should always try to intercept a pass to the player they are marking.

In this scenario, player A passes toward his teammate, player B. Player C, the defender, practices stepping in front of player B and intercepts the pass. Player C then passes the ball to the next player in the serving line and play continues. At this stage, players A and B are playing at 50 percent of full effort, ensuring that player C is getting the opportunity to win the ball each time.

Defenders focus on establishing a strong physical position (get a shoulder-ahead) and then controlling the run of the attacker using their arms (make oneself wide) to keep the attacker at bay. A variation here is to have the servers toss balls in the air for the defender to win.

DEFENDING FOOTWORK: PRIORITIES (2A)— DENY TURN

If the defending player is unable to win the ball outright, his next priority is to *deny the turn*. The diagram shows the new, staggered start positions of players B and C, which will allow the attacker (B) to get to the ball first.

In this situation, the defender still has some advantages as the attacker is not particularly dangerous on the ball if he is facing away from the goal.

DEFENDING FOOTWORK: PRIORITIES (2B)— DENY TURN

sports-graphics.com

To deny the turn to the attacker, the defender (B), gets "touch-close" to the attacker.

At this stage, once again, players A and B are working to help player C achieve success. Thus, player B does not try to turn, but rather dribbles slowly to either circled area where the simulation ends and the ball is returned to the serving line. Be certain to rotate roles.

DEFENDING FOOTWORK: PRIORITIES (3A)— DENY PENETRATION

If the defender cannot deny the ball or the turn to the attacker, his next priority is to *deny penetration*. In this scenario, the starting position of the defender (C) is moved to a more disadvantageous position, allowing the pass from A to B to create time for B to face up with the goal before the defender (C) arrives.

DEFENDING FOOTWORK: PRIORITIES (3B)— DENY PENETRATION

Given that the defender cannot deny the ball or the turn, he closes down and forces the attacker to dribble laterally, pushing him to a sharper angle and staying close enough to interfere with a shot attempt.

Player B, the attacker, again plays with the understanding that he should allow himself to be forced off to either circled area, and then he should return the ball to the serving line. Rotate roles.

DEFENDING FOOTWORK: PRIORITIES (4)— DENY SHOT

sports-graphics.com

The final choice for the defender—if he is unable to deny the ball, the turn, or penetrative dribbling to the attacker—is to work to deny the shot. Note that the starting position for the defender (C) has been stretched to put him in a very disadvantageous location. B should be able to check, receive, turn, and dribble toward goal before C can arrive. In this case, the defender gets in between the attacker and the goal and then tries to drive the attacker to a poorer shooting angle while simultaneously getting close enough to block or at least interfere with the attacker's shot attempt.

As in the previous examples, it is advisable to allow the attacker to increase his effort gradually. In other words, allow the defender to close down and guide the attacker to a poor shooting angle before letting him block a shot attempt, and then encourage the attackers to increase their effort and speed until the exercise is wide open.

DEFENDING FOOTWORK: SEPARATING OPPONENT FROM THE BALL

sports-graphics.com

Excellent preparatory footwork may allow the defender to avoid tackling altogether. In this exercise, the attacker must receive the pass from his teammate and take a touch in the direction of the open cone. The attacker, to start, should be fairly passive in their role. The defender observes the attacker's first touch and then separates him from the ball by being quicker into the space as shown and then using his physical presence in the space to win the ball. Players rotate positions and roles after each repetition.

This action, when possible, is less likely to produce a foul and allows the defender to win the ball cleanly off the attacker's touch rather than tackling and then running down the loose ball.

The exercise can be progressed to allow the attacker to play harder and to have a free first touch regarding direction. Finally, a grid can be built around the duelers, and they can play to end lines as in many of the proceeding drills. The idea here is to build recognition and skill in the defender to seize the moment when the ball is out of the feet of the attacker.

DEFENDING FOOTWORK: SEPARATING OPPONENT FROM THE BALL IN A LIVE EXERCISE

sports-graphics.com

This simple exercise takes the technique described in the previous drill to a live environment. In a relatively small grid (to create more opportunities to confront an attacker), half the players start with a ball. Those players dribble around, and the players without the ball look for the right moment to intervene, stepping between the attacker and the ball, and using their bodies, and within the rules, their arms, to establish a primary position on the ball. The coach should specify that, in this exercise, no tackling is allowed. Rather, defenders must rely on decisive footwork, timing and the use of their bodies to win the ball. For the first minute, instruct players on a ball to allow defenders to come and win the ball from them, then empower the attackers to fight to keep their ball.

Freiburg's Lucas Höler (right) separates Leverkusen's Odilon Kossounou from the ball.
(picture alliance/dpa | Philipp von Ditfurth)

DEFENDING FOOTWORK: CLOSE DOWN AND RECOVER

Closing down is critical to the success of individual defending. Too slow and shallow, and the attacker maintains her options for too long. Too quick, deep, and out of control, and the attacker may be able to get in behind. The defender must therefore learn to balance speed with control, using longer, quick steps to close the distance along with an angle designed to limit the attacker's options. As the defender approaches the attacker, she must shorten her steps to be able to make quick adjustments. Posture is also critical here. If the defender gets her weight out beyond her lead foot or is leaning onto the back foot, she will be poorly balanced, again limiting her ability to adjust. During the back pedal phase, maintain focus on the ball in front.

The lead player closes down the three mannequins as shown, each time getting set for 1 second before backpedaling to the center. After closing down and recovering from the third ball, she sprints through the gate at right. Then next player jumps in after the player in front has begun her sprint.

DEFENDING FOOTWORK: BLOCK TACKLE

This environment allows players to practice closing down and block tackling. Block tackling is a difficult skill for young players, and for more experienced players, it is a technique that requires frequent practice to refine movement and also timing. The active player closes down toward the gate. At the gate, the player sets his footwork and pauses before recognizing that the ball is in or near the feet of the attacker, whose role here is to provide a good tackling partner for the working player. The active player then moves to block tackle, trapping the ball between the opponent's foot and his own.

Emphasize:

- Get the plant foot close enough to the ball to ensure good balance and also to be able to control the ball (a wide stance may allow the ball to go between the defender's feet and behind).

- Lock the ankle on the tackling foot.

- Toes up, heel down to help control the ball.

- Knee over the ball to keep it from popping up at the moment of the tackle.

- Stay goal side of the ball (no walk-through).

Hold the tackle for 3 seconds. Then the working player back-pedals around the next cone before closing down through the gate, setting his feet and then block tackling the second attacker as shown. Note that the defender alternates his angle of approach so that he can also switch the tackling foot. Finally, the defender makes a recovery sprint through the last gate before jogging back to the start point.

It's a good idea to have extra soccer balls nearby as sometimes the tackling will cause a ball to be pushed away, and having a replacement handy will facilitate more efficient training.

Sei Muroya (left) of Hannover block tackles Ingolstadt's Nils Röseler.
(picture alliance/dpa | Stefan Puchner)

DEFENDING FOOTWORK: POKE TACKLE (1)

With an eye toward efficiency and isolating this important skill, this practice allows defenders to focus on closing down, poke tackling, and then scoring after winning the ball. The defender (1) passes to the attacker (2), and then closes down. The attacker's role in the exercise is simply to provide the opportunity for the defender to poke tackle.

DEFENDING FOOTWORK: POKE TACKLE (2)

In this second drill, the action of creating the poke tackle opportunity is highlighted. The attacker takes dribbling touches in the direction of the cone at the bottom of the area. The defender has closed down and proceeds to jockey the attacker, looking for the moment to tackle.

Observe:

• Poke tackle when the ball is not at the feet of the attacker.

• Use a quick, decisive poking motion to push the ball away from the attacker.

• If using the front foot to tackle, the defender will be able to disguise the tackle better, but there is a greater risk of fouling as well. It's important to try to avoid any contact with the attacker if possible.

• If using the back foot to tackle, the defender must understand this technique is more difficult to disguise but easier to avoid fouling (longer reach to tackle).

- Defenders should also understand that if the tackling motion results in shifting weight to the front foot, the defender may have difficulty recovering quickly if the tackle is missed. Players should try to maintain good balance to recover as fast as possible if necessary.

- Tap the ball out of the path of the attacker and then run through onto the ball.

After tackling, the defender should then dribble at speed through the gate and pass the ball into the goal. Players change roles and repeat the exercise. The exercise should also be altered to reverse the angle of serve and approach so the defenders become accustomed to working both ways and with either foot.

SC Freiburg's Nicolas Höfler (left) pokes the ball away from Leverkusen's Amine Adli.
(picture alliance/dpa | Philipp von Ditfurth)

DEFENDING FOOTWORK: SLIDE TACKLE

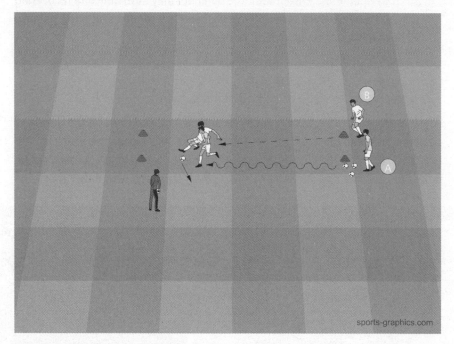

sports-graphics.com

Slide tackling is the final, least-preferred form of tackle. The drawbacks to this type of tackle are that it requires the defender to leave his feet, meaning that if he is unsuccessful, the defender will be out of the play until he recovers his feet. In addition, particularly at the youth levels, referees are more inclined to call a foul—earned or not—when a defender slide tackles. Thus, a defender making a dramatic slide tackle may win the ball but incur a free kick or penalty kick against his team. Finally, because the defender ends up lying prone on the ground with the attacker running through, there is greater possibility for injury. For all of these reasons, slide tackling should be considered an emergency maneuver, only used when poke or block tackling are not possible.

When should a defender slide tackle? If the attacker gets behind the defender in their duel, and the defender is confident he will not be able to recover to a goal-side position, slide tackling can be effective.

In the diagram, players practice slide tackling in a controlled environment under the supervision of the coach. The attacker (A) dribbles from the start cone toward the destination cone. The defender (B) pursues. At this stage, the attacker should move at about half speed, helping the defender throughout to experiment with and refine his technique.

To slide tackle, the defender must move close enough to reach the ball with the tackle. Always tackle when the ball is out of the attacker's feet (i.e., after a touch). The defender slides on his nearside (to the opponent) hip, being careful to keep his hands at his sides for balance, and also keeping them away from the attacker to avoid fouling or being stepped on.

The defender looks to either tap the ball out of the path of the attacker (using either foot), or trap the ball in place so that when the attacker makes his next touch, the ball will remain corralled between them (usually using the away foot so there can be downward pressure on the ball with the foot in a raised position, near back-center of the ball). The momentum of the attacker will usually cause him to stumble past the ball.

It is crucial that the defender contacts the ball first and limits any contact with the attacker to avoid fouling or incurring injury.

Gradually increase the speed and freedom of the attacker, adding a goal to play to in the final progression.

*Stuttgart's Philipp Förster (left) slide tackles Munich's Kingsley Coman.
(picture alliance/dpa | Tom Weller)*

1V1: KNOCK OUT

Often used as a warm-up activity, this exercise is fun and also challenging for players of any age. Each player has a ball, and they dribble around the area, trying to protect their ball and simultaneously knock other players' balls out of the grid. Players receive a point for each ball they knock out of the area. If a player's ball is knocked out of the area, they must run after it and then do touch-work (i.e., 10 dribbles or juggles) before reentering. The coach can observe tackling and reinforce exemplary block and poke tackling.

To raise the intensity and the stakes, remove several balls from the area. Players still receive a point for sending other players' balls out of the area, but they are disqualified in the final score check if they have not won and kept a ball.

DEFENDING FOOTWORK: KNEE TAG

Players duel, keeping track of the number of times they can touch their opponent's knees. Duels last 15 seconds. Players cannot run away, though they may move back and forth in a small space. The opponent's hand can be blocked, but the player cannot turn away. Try this exercise once and then ask players how this is similar to individual defending.

Responses should include:

• Posture: players must get low to protect themselves and also be quick to tag.

• Stance: showing both knees to the opponent will inevitably lead to conceding points. It is important in the real game to only show one knee to the opponent to limit that player's options.

• Footwork: as in the real game, the players need to be able to quickly move forward and back with chopping steps to adjust to their opponent's moves.

- Fakes: part of disrupting the attacker in a duel is getting that player to focus on protecting the ball rather than his attacking options. In this game, sharp fakes to tag put the other player in a defensive mind frame.

Play four to five duels, rotating partners after each match.

DEFENDING FOOTWORK: BALL TAG

Players work in pairs with one ball. The attacker uses her feet to control and move the ball. She cannot run away and must try to protect the ball using her body and quick movement of the ball. The defender uses her hands to try to tag the ball. She cannot foul the attacker, though she can apply physical pressure and try to move the attacker to reach the ball.

This game teaches defenders to focus on the ball and to use their feet to gain access to the ball. Defenders will have to be aggressive and get physical contact with the attacker, trying to manipulate and anticipate her movements. Defenders should work from jockeying position throughout, and they cannot leave their feet. One potential bad habit that can be exacerbated in this setting is the tendency for the defender to adopt a posture that is not well-balanced. For example, in looking to reach for the ball, many defenders get their heads out in front of their feet, which can lead the player to overcommit in the game. Monitor the defender's posture and encourage them to stay balanced as they work.

Play for 20 seconds and then change roles. If the defender tags the ball, the duel restarts until time expires. Play four duels and then change partners.

DEFENDING FOOTWORK: CLOSE DOWN AND CONTROL IN A GRID

This setup is similar to a standard 1v1 training exercise. The defender passes the ball to the attacker and then closes down. The defender cannot tackle in this exercise! The goal of the defender is to either force the attacker out of the grid on either side or delay her as long as possible. The attacker must try to dribble out the end of the grid where the defender started. These restrictions compel the defender to focus on using an effective angle to close down, with quick feet and physical pressure to limit the options and speed of the attacker. Players change ends and roles after each duel.

DUELING: WINNING 1V1 DUELS

1V1 CONTINUOUS

This is the basic environment for training individual defending. With minor adjustments, this setting can be manipulated to emphasize every aspect of individual defending. In the base exercise, the defender serves to the attacker, who tries to dribble over the defender's end line to win the duel. If the defender wins the ball, she tries to dribble over the attacker's end line to win the duel.

At the conclusion of the duel (when the ball leaves the grid), the players change ends and roles and play continues.

Coach:

- Closing down. The defender must always work to limit the attacker's options. Work to get the attacker's head down and then increase the pressure.

- Be physical. This should be a difficult moment for any attacker as they are stuck in a small space against a focused defender. Getting a shoulder into the attacker whenever she moves laterally is very important to the defender's success.

- Patience. The longer the duel lasts, the more likely the defender will have help in the real game. Accordingly, defenders should work to delay the attacker and find a moment to tackle. Rushing in and overcommitting is a common reason players lose duels.

- Use fakes. Faking to try to get the ball helps the defender get control of the situation, disrupting the attacker's sense of control in the duel.

- Never quit. If the ball is inside the grid, the players must continue to duel.

- A word about mentality. Note in the previous example, the defender does not pass the ball right to the attacker. There is no reason to be nice in this situation, even in training. The goal here is to win the duel, and the attacker should be passed into a corner and then isolated there until the ball is won.

1V1 "KILL TOUCH"

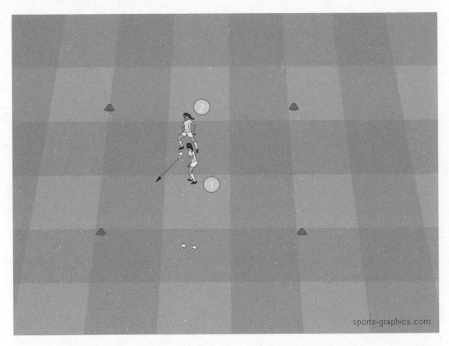

sports-graphics.com

Duels often evolve to a critical moment wherein the attacker (2) attempts a "kill touch," which is an effort to push the ball behind the defender (1) and then get the next touch. The defender's response at this moment will decide the outcome of the duel.

1V1 "SWIMMING" TO WIN THE DUEL

In this drill, the defender moves to separate the attacker (2) from the ball. The key components of this move are:

• Get into the path from the attacker to the ball.

• Make shoulder contact and get "shoulder-ahead." In most cases, the player whose shoulder is closer to the ball at this moment will win the duel.

• If necessary, "swim" to gain the upper hand. Bringing one's arm over the top and then in front of the opponent, in essence a swimming motion, will limit the speed and ability of the attacker to reach the ball. It's important to remember that extending the arm can create a foul, and that there is a "gray" area where quality defenders learn to work, limiting their opponent's movement without earning a whistle.

Hoffenheim's Katharina Naschenweng (right) works to get shoulder-ahead of Arsenal's Beth Mead.
(picture alliance/dpa | Uwe Anspach)

1V1 IMMEDIATE PRESSURE

This exercise is a great means of helping defenders understand the importance and benefits of immediate pressure. The defender (1) serves to the attacker (2) and then moves to close down. Note that the defender is advised to put the ball in the corner for the attacker and then move to isolate him in that space. Point out to the defender that it's much easier to defend and win the ball in the small corner space than chase the attacker around the whole grid.

Mentality matters here again as well. Many defenders will play a friendly pass to the attacker where the latter player starts unless they are conditioned that the goal here is to win the duel, not to make the attacker comfortable. Pushing a ball into the corner immediately places the attacker in an unenviable situation, and then getting high pressure further complicates the attacker's position.

The attacker attempts to dribble out of the bottom of the grid. If the defender wins the ball, he dribbles out the top of the grid. Play until the ball leaves the area and then change roles.

Another tip here is to gradually move the defender's starting position further away from the attacker's line and to vary the start point. For instance, the start cone could be placed in the center of the grid. In this way, the defender's understanding of space and angles evolves, helping him to know what is required to deal with attackers who approach from different distances and angles.

1V1 IMMEDIATE PRESSURE WITH SERVER

This exercise is based on the same idea as the previous drill, except that there is now a server to initiate the duel, and the defender enters from the other side of the grid. The server can give a more friendly, central serve to the attacker and make the timing more challenging for the defender, who still has a relatively short distance to cover to close down. The defender will face an incrementally more difficult challenge as the attacker cannot be immediately locked in a corner, and this helps evolve the defender's sense of creating pressure. If she goes flying in without thought, the attacker may get behind her right away. Conversely, if the defender is too cautious, she will lose the advantage of her close starting position. As with all aspects of dueling, it is a matter of managing variables, from distance and the presence of the boundaries to the quality of touches by the attacker, and then learning and refining one's own abilities, that creates a formula for success here.

1V1 TO A SIDE CONE GOAL

sports-graphics.com

This is a useful environment for showing individual defenders the importance of directional defending. The defender passes to the attacker, who tries to dribble through the side cone goal. The goal is small and located to the side to compel the defender to focus on denying specific space to the attacker. Thus, the defender's approach and tackling must be calculated to keep the attacker as far from the goal as possible. This situation is clearly analogous to many situations in the game, particularly to an outside back dealing with an attacker on the flank. It is useful to limit the time available to the attacker (i.e., 10 seconds) to encourage that player to take risks, and reward the defender if he can contain the attacker. If the attacker wins the ball, he should try to dribble out the top side of the grid. Change roles after each duel.

1V1 TO TWO SIDE CONE GOALS

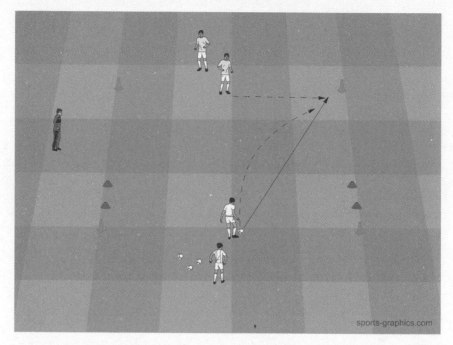

Adding a second cone goal, as shown in the diagram, complicates the work of the defender, who must now focus on using a fast, but controlled approach and physical pressure to keep the attacker at bay and away from the goals at the bottom of the grid. The attacker can win by dribbling through either cone goal. The defender tries to win the ball and dribble out the attacker's end of the grid. If the attacker is able to penetrate to the bottom half of the grid, the defender will have a difficult time in defending both goals. He must therefore try to keep the attacker near the latter's starting point.

1V1 CALL START

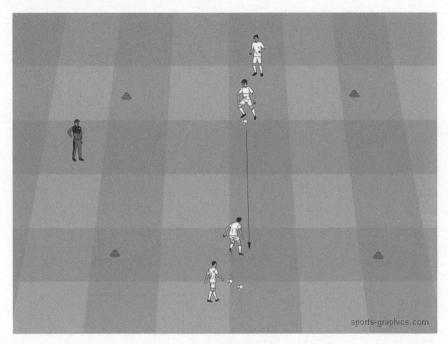

sports-graphics.com

In this variant, the two active players knock a ball (1-touch). After a handful of passes, the next player in the server line hollers, "Go!" and the duel begins, with both players trying to win the ball and dribble over their opponent's end line. Play until the ball leaves the area. This environment compels the players to be ready for either the defending or attacking role at the outset, and it makes the start random, much as duels are commenced in a match.

1V1 THROW-IN

This is a standard dueling exercise, except that each duel starts with a throw-in. This requirement teaches the defending player to assess the touch of the attacker to decide whether to immediately tackle. The phrase coaches use in this situation is "on his/her touch!," which reminds players to close down knowing that if the attacker's first touch is long, the defender may be able to immediately move to win the ball. Another important consideration here is if the attacker's first touch puts the ball underneath him, he will need at least two more touches to move the ball. Therefore, the defender may consider tackling immediately as well, knowing that the attacker will be preoccupied and trying to find a safe outlet. Finally, if the attacker's first touch is negative, the defender should get "touch-tight" and compel the attacker to duel with his back to the goal (line) he is trying to play toward.

Players try to dribble over their opponents' end line and then switch roles and ends for the next duel.

Hoffenheim's Kevin Vogt (left) closes down Gladbach's Breel Embolo, reading the attacker's first touch out of the air.
(picture alliance/dpa | Uwe Anspach)

1V1 LONG GRID WITH LONG PASS

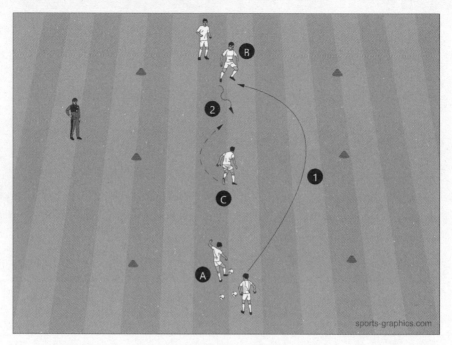

This environment places additional technical demands on more experienced players. Player A passes long to player B, sending his pass over player C in the middle of the grid. Player B settles the ball and then tries to get past player C. B wins the duel if he can dribble over the grid end line at the bottom of the area. Player C, meanwhile, tries to close down player B and steal the ball. To win the duel, C must dribble over the end line at the top of the grid. Play continues until the ball leaves the grid area. Player rotation is as follows: A to C, C to B's line, and B to A's line.

Coach:

• Long passing. Can players chip or loft a ball over a standing obstruction to a target?

• Receiving. A poor first touch will put the attacker in a difficult position against an aggressive defender.

- Closing down. The defender's starting position in the middle of the grid places him in a bit of a precarious spot. Encourage the defender to react to the quality of the first touch of the attacker. If the attacker is unable to control the ball cleanly with his first touch, the defender should attempt to intervene and win the ball immediately. This is often referred to as being "on (his) touch," a useful reminder for a situation that occurs frequently in every match.

- Dealing with an attacker in larger space. Because of the length of the grid (recommend 20 x 10 yards), the attacker has some room to maneuver, and if he uses a change of speed, he may be able to exploit the space behind the defender. The defender must be aware of this space and use caution if the attacker gains early control of the ball. The grid is still fairly narrow, so the defender must try to force the attacker to one side, limiting the room for maneuver. If he can pinch the attacker to the sideline of the grid, the defender has a better chance to then absorb the speed of the attacker and take the ball off him.

- Recovery runs. Because of the length of the grid, if one player manages to get behind an opponent, there is still time to recover. Demand that players continue to play until the ball leaves the area.

1V1 CHIP

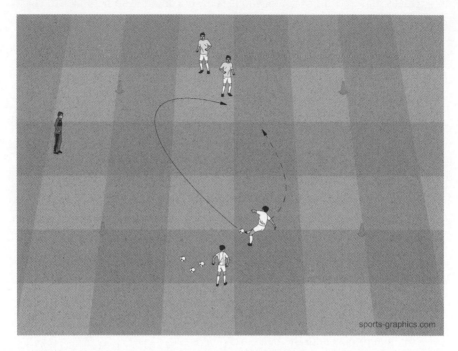

The duel starts with a chipped serve by the defender to the attacker. Both players try to dribble over their opponent's end line. The chipped serve places technical demands on both the defender and the attacker, whose receiving touch will influence the behavior of the defender at the outset. The defender should be prepared to close quickly if the attacker's touch is long, negative, or places the ball underneath him. If the attacker settles the ball cleanly, the defender must close more cautiously and work to contain the attacker's dribbling, looking for the moment to tackle.

1V1 JUGGLE AND VOLLEY

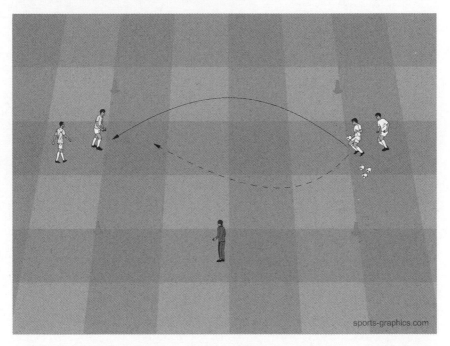

In this instance, the defender juggles the ball 4–5 touches and then volleys the ball to the attacker to initiate the duel. The defender's approach is dictated by the quality of the attacker's receiving touch. If the attacker's touch is long, negative, or places the ball between his feet, the defender should look to close quickly and win the duel right away. If the attacker's touch is clean, the defender must look to contain the attacker's dribbling and find a moment to win the ball.

1V1 BACK-TO-BACK

Duelers stand back-to-back at the center of the grid with a ball trapped between them, as shown. At a signal from the coach, the players let the ball fall and the duel commences. The players must let the ball touch the ground before they can play it. Each player attempts to win the ball and dribble over their opponent's end line.

Given that 1v1 training is fundamental to building a successful team-defending philosophy, this environment and others included here are designed to keep the training fresh and challenging, as well as fun for the players. The coach can augment these exercises by adding competitive elements, particularly by keeping score.

1V1 TO A CENTER CONE/BALL GOAL

The defender line (1) passes a ball anywhere in the grid for the first member of the attacker line (2) to run onto and initiate the duel. The attacker is allowed the first touch, and she tries to use the ball to knock the other ball off the cone/ball goal at the center of the grid. The defender tries to win the ball and dribbles out any side of the grid. Then the players change lines and the next duel begins.

This is an especially challenging environment because of the small, central target. The defender learns to defend a particular point, placing her body between the attacker and the cone/ball goal. These duels usually result in much physical pressure for both players as they battle for position in the limited space.

1V1 2 CONE BALL GOALS

Here a server pushes balls randomly into the grid for the two players to chase down. Each player now defends a cone/ball goal and tries to knock the ball off their opponent's goal. In addition to being another fun 1v1 variant, this exercise helps defenders learn about defending from all angles and trying to protect a particular point. Once again, the players must decide on the serve from the coach, whether to go after the ball immediately or adopt a defensive posture to protect their goal. Play until a goal is scored or the ball leaves the grid.

1V1 TO A CENTRAL STICK GOAL

sports-graphics.com

Here the defender starts the duel in the central goal by passing to the attacker along the perimeter. The attacker must try to dribble through the center goal from either side. The defender tries to win the ball and dribble out of the grid on any side.

This is another example of an individual defending exercise designed to help young players in particular appreciate the importance of defending space, as the attacker has the option of running at the goal from any direction, while the defender, though anchored to defense of the goal, must both defend from all angles and also find a way to win the ball. The defender will learn patience and the importance of recognizing and trying to seize the initiative in the duel. The attacker has many advantages but, ultimately, must try to beat the defender, and the latter must play for the moment when he will have a chance to win the ball. Defenders will often try to seize the initiative by playing aggressively, and this strategy can lead to a win but also carries much risk if the defender fails to win the ball. These calculations are central to learning the individual defending role.

1V1 50/50 BALL

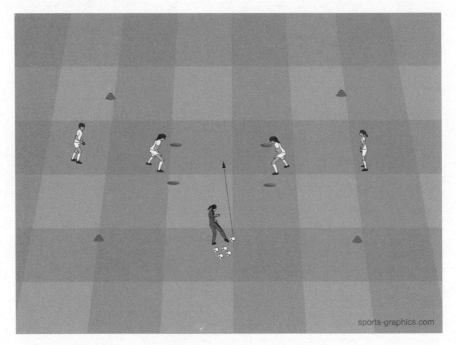

The two players move up to the edge of the inner grid, as shown. They must stay on the perimeter of that area until the ball is served by the coach. The players then try to win the ball and dribble over their opponent's end line. This is a good way to teach players to recognize a 50/50 ball and improve their ability to judge their best response in these situations. Can they win the ball immediately? If they are too aggressive, their opponent may win the ball and the duel very quickly. If, on the other hand, they are too cautious, they may end up playing defense every time. The coach can complicate the environment by playing serves in the air or with varied pace.

1V1 TO SMALL GOALS: SPEED

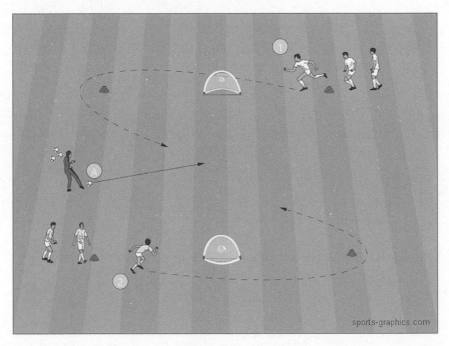

The coach serves balls (A) into the grid for two players. Players 1 and 2 must run along the end lines of the grid, rounding the far corners, as shown, and then try to get to the ball first. Both players try to win the ball and then score in their opponent's goal.

This environment is an excellent means of teaching players how to deal with 50/50 ball situations. Until the players enter the grid it is unknown who will have the best chance to arrive at the ball first and, therefore, players have to become attuned to both approaching quickly and also making split-second decisions as to whether they should go full speed to win the ball, or, if there is a chance they will be beaten to the ball, decide on a more conservative entry, assuring they will be able to defend their goal and have a chance to win the ball from their opponent. These situations occur frequently in the real game, and thus this is a useful means of isolating and tuning that particular decision-making process.

This game also engenders a competitive spirit in 1v1 training, with the players' dueling abilities on display in front of coaches and teammates.

1V1 DEFENDER CHASE

The defender (1) passes to attacker (2), who tries to dribble out the top of the grid. The defender must chase down the attacker, win the ball, and then dribble over the start line at the bottom of the grid.

The task here is for the defender to learn to battle to get goal side, deflect or stop the attacker's dribbling, and then duel to win the ball. The defender will learn to be physical in trying to distract and then shut down the attacker's run, and the use of the "swimming" technique (getting shoulder-ahead) is necessary.

There is often a tendency for the defender to cheat a bit here—leaving early, passing to the rear foot of the defender, or playing the ball very slowly. The coach must ensure that the pass is properly weighted to the front foot of the attacker, and neither player can leave early. Many coaches use this setting to teach and refine slide tackling.

Change roles after each duel.

1V1 RECOVERY DUELS

Players 1 and 2 play a standard duel to end lines (A). Then both players must go and touch a designated cone on their defensive end of the grid (B, C). The coach then passes a ball to a random location in the grid, and the players duel again to end lines.

This drill introduces the concept of recovery runs, which are critical to in-depth defensive scheming. Standard dueling exercises engender a sense of play and then rest that is often absent in the real game. Win or lose, the player is often required to move on to the next tactical demand in the game. Any laziness or hesitancy in this regard can be fatal to the defensive structure and culture of the team. This exercise combats the onset of that mentality by forcing players to make a recovery run after their duel and then participate in another contest.

1V1 TWO GRIDS

sports-graphics.com

Players duel against an opponent in a grid, trying to win and keep the ball. The player in possession, after a minimum of five touches, tries to pass to the other member of his team in the adjacent grid. Because there are no goals, this environment emphasizes physical duels as the players look to protect the ball and find a moment to transfer the ball to the other grid. Encourage defenders to get between their opponent and the other grid, and then pressure the opponent, driving him to corners and the back of the grid and tackling when the right moment appears. This environment has the benefits of some built-in rest for players when the ball is in the other grid, though players must still try to maneuver to receive a pass from their teammate.

1V1 FOUR GOALS

sports-graphics.com

The coach plays balls into the grid in a random fashion. The active player from each group enters the grid and defends the two goals on her end line while trying to score in either of her opponent's goals.

This exercise helps players deal with situations where they are uncertain about their role (attack or defend?) until the ball is played into the area. They also have to make decisions about how to defend two goals. As defender, it is very useful to try to get tight to the attacker and force her to face away from the goals, trying to cut off her path to either goal. If the attacker is able to face the goals, the defender needs to cut off the direct path to the nearest goal and then try to increase pressure by closing down. The defender also needs to become more adept at defending in space in this exercise, understanding that overcommitting to defending one goal may result in her being beaten to the other goal. Thus, the defender will learn to balance pressure and patience to win the duel.

1V1 TO GOAL

Player 1 serves to player 2, who must dribble past player 1 before he can shoot at the goal. If player 1 wins control of the ball, the duel ends. After the duel, the players change lines. Then player 3 serves to player 4, and the exercise continues.

Coach:

- The defender must cover a lot of ground to shut down the attacker. Emphasize speed after the ball is served, allowing the defender to meet and challenge the attacker further up the field, away from the goal.

- The angle of approach is very important. In general, defenders try to push the attacker away from the center of the field and to a poorer shooting angle. It is important to strike the right balance between pushing the attacker wide and not allowing that player to dribble freely to goal.

- This is a good environment in which to emphasize goalkeeper communication. The goalkeeper should coach the defender throughout, encouraging him to prevent a shot, push the attacker wide, clear a loose ball, etc.

1V1 CONTINUOUS TO GOAL

sports-graphics.com

Attacker 1 tries to dribble past the defender (2) and score in goal A. If player 2 wins the ball, the duel ends. As soon as the duel is concluded, player 3 attacks goal B and player 1 becomes the defender. Play continues with players joining alternately as attackers and then defending in a duel against an attacker from the other end. Players return to the line from which they joined the exercise.

In addition to adding realism through an attack on goal, this exercise highlights the importance of transition as the attacker must quickly switch to defending at the end of his attacking effort. Many players will forget to defend and leave their goalkeeper alone to face the attacker from the other team. This is a powerful reminder that the player that failing to defend is letting down his team.

Tactically, this is a challenging environment in that the attacker will be close to the goal, and the defender will likely be in a poor position to start the duel. The defender must endeavor to get goal side and apply pressure to the attacker and try to drive him away from the goal and to a poor shooting angle.

It should be noted that the coach may need to use a restriction to allow the new defender at least a moment to get in position, particularly in the early moments of the exercise. For instance, the coach can require a certain number of touches by the attacker before he can go forward after the conclusion of the previous duel. Another means of creating a more fair initiation of each duel is for the new attacker to pass the ball to the new defender, who then returns the ball to the attacker, and the duel begins. Finally, the new attacker can be required to do some physical work (i.e., a burpee, or two lunges in place) before charging into the area. Regardless, the crucial point of assessment for the coach is to find the balance of giving the defender sufficient time to get to the attacker while also creating time pressure for the defender to hustle.

1V1 BOX DUELS

The coach pushes a ball into the 18-yard box. Wherever it rolls to a stop, one player from each team approaches the ball and stands 1 yard away. The coach calls out a color or name, and that player becomes the attacker, trying to score in the full-sized goal. The other player tries to win the ball and score in either of the small goals. Both players are live from the call of the coach. Play until the ball leaves the area.

Variations:

- The attacker gets one free touch, but the defender can move right away to a goal-side position.

- The ball is live from the moment the coach passed it into the area, and the first player to touch it becomes the player attacking the full-sized goal.

1V1 DEFENDING "FLAT" NEAR THE GOAL

Player C passes in to player A, who tries to score past defender B and the goalkeeper. The defender starts the sequence at the dot placed 10 yards from goal. The attacker is allowed a receiving touch before the defender becomes active. The attacker will try to face up with the goal, and the defender should try to prevent that turn. Play until the defender gains possession or clears the area, a goal by the attacker, or 10 seconds expires.

Defending near the goal against a faced-up attacker, particularly from straight on, requires special consideration by the defender. Ordinarily, defenders are encouraged to use footwork that allows them to shade an opponent to one side, guiding the attacker to predictable behavior and space. It's important to point out that doing so from straight on to goal will result in shots and likely goals, as the attacker will use any open look at goal to try to finish. Therefore, the defender should be shown how to defend "flat," not favoring either side, if the attacker is near the goal and approaching from a fairly straight angle. Note that if the approach is from a sharper angle (i.e., the side of the 6-yard box), the defender would be encouraged to drive the attacker to an even more difficult angle, i.e., the end line.

By defending "flat" and closing to within 2 yards of the attacker, as well as menacing that player with aggressive posture, the defender presents the best possible scenario under the circumstances for blocking the attacker's shot and route to goal. In the "flat" posture, the defender is vulnerable to being beaten to either side, as well as between her feet, and she must be careful to avoid committing a handball foul in the case of a shot. The hope, however, is that a shot is discouraged or blocked and that the attacker pauses, allowing additional defenders to descend upon the attacker and dispossess her. The 10-second limit on the length of the duel is important because it encourages the defender to delay the attacker, theoretically buying time for her teammates to assist. The restriction also places pressure on the attacker to play at game speed, creating better training conditions.

Another useful piece of advice in this situation is to teach the defender to "match and mirror" the footwork of the attacker. In other words, if the attacker takes three steps to her right, the defender should take three steps to her left, using the same stride, while also slightly closing the distance, particularly if the touch is at all negative (away from goal) in angle. In this way, her mirrored footwork should help keep her in a position to block a shot attempt.

1V1 BOGIE ALLEY

sports-graphics.com

Often used as a warm-up exercise for young players, Bogie alley is a fun, intensive 1v1 training environment. The defenders, usually 1 or 1 fewer in number than attackers, are isolated in a rectangular grid (roughly 15 x 22 for 9–10 players). The defenders earn a point for every ball they knock out of the grid. Attackers earn one point for dribbling across the grid and two points for navigating the long (top to bottom) route through the grid. Defenders may not focus on one attacker. Attackers may not remain outside the grid for more than 10 seconds. If attackers lose their ball, they run to retrieve it and try again. Play for 2 minutes and then change the defenders.

Coaches can watch this exercise to assess the 1v1 defending of their players and whether footwork, tackling, and dueling training are visible in an environment more fluid than a grid.

1V1 CORNER DUELS

Divide the team equally among four stations (1–4) near small corner goals. Player 1 passes to player 2 (A) and then closes down (B). Player 2 tries to score in player 1's goal, while player 1 wants to win the ball and pass it through the goal defended by player 2's team. The duel continues until the ball leaves the area. When the duel ends, the two players change lines. Then player 3 serves to player 4, and those two players carry on a similar duel, trying to pass the ball through their opponent's goal.

It is important to keep the numbers in each group small in this setting because it is otherwise inefficient. However, it does put each player's dueling on display for the group and the added pressure can increase competitive intensity, allowing the coach to observe, influence, and emphasize the team's 1v1 culture.

1V1 LADDER

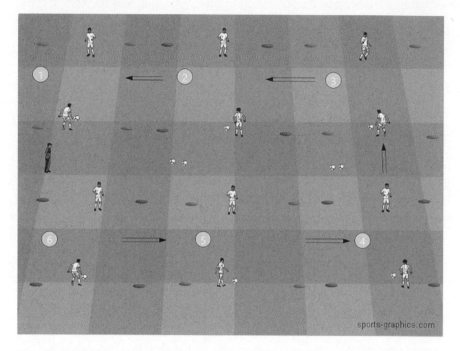

The 1v1 ladder is a means of assessing players' 1v1 abilities and their competitive instincts. Set up grids with safety zones, as shown, building half the number of grids of the total player count. Place extra balls in the center safety zone between grid lines. Send players in pairs to a grid with a ball, as shown.

All players compete simultaneously, with duels lasting 30–40 seconds. Duels start and restart after the ball leaves the area with a pass across the grid. Players earn a point each time they dribble over their opponent's end line. When a point is scored, the player scoring passes to the other player to restart.

At the conclusion of each round of duels, players who win move up the ladder one grid (the winner in the top grid stays put), and those losing their duels move down the ladder one rung (the player in the bottom grid also stays where he is). If there are an odd number of players, the player losing in the bottom grid can step out and juggle through the next duel before reentering the bottom grid to duel again.

In the case of a draw, the player who scored first wins. If there is no score, the player in possession at the conclusion of time wins. If there is no score and the ball is out of the grid at the conclusion of the duel, the players play one round of Rock, Paper, Scissors to determine a winner.

It is important to play enough rounds to allow those beginning at the bottom of the grid to reach the top and win the competition.

This is an outstanding exercise for player evaluation, as the coaches will have an opportunity to test the dueling abilities as well as the fitness and mental toughness of their players.

It is also important to note, however, that this experience can be discouraging for players who struggle. It is advisable to emphasize that this is a "lab" of sorts for players to work on their dueling, and that if one struggles, it simply means that one should spend more time dueling and be ready to climb the ladder next time.

1V1 DENY PASS

An excellent environment to train players' understanding of how to deny a through pass or cross, this exercise compels defenders to think about spacing and the importance of positioning with regard to the ball when dueling. The defender initiates play by passing to the attacker (see diagram). Both players must remain on their side of the three cone gates. The attacker dribbles to try to find an open gate. Then he passes through the gate, trying to knock the ball off one of the cone/ball goals. The attacker is limited to 15 seconds to make his effort, and if he misses or is blocked before that, the duel ends. An interesting variation or progression here is to compel the attacker to get beyond the cone before passing, thus allowing the defender to block the effort or tackle. Change roles.

Coach:

- Posture and speed. Is the defender able to challenge and intimidate the defender without being able to tackle? Think about the footwork required for movement—specifically, longer strides to cover more space and when the ball is not in the feet of the attacker, and shorter strides when in tighter space (to be able to make adjustments) and when the attacker is in close control of the ball. The exercise also highlights the risky nature of lunging to block the ball. Lunging and shifting weight to the blocking foot can commit the defender to the movement, freeing the attacker to get an advantage working to another goal. The defender must only commit when he is confident that blocking will be necessary and successful.

- Can the defender anticipate and deny the goal to the attacker without overcommitting?

- Fakes. The defender, if he stays in the vision of the attacker, can fake to push ahead, forcing a change of plan and direction by the attacker.

1V1 DENY CROSS

An often neglected aspect of individual defending involves helping players understand the considerations in denying crosses. In this exercise, player 1 passes to player 2. Player 2 then tries to cross the ball from inside of the cone grid. The only additional restriction on the attacker is that he must dribble forward past the stick posted outside of the area. He may subsequently cut the ball back and cross from the start-side of the stick. The restriction prevents the attacker from crossing first time, allowing the defender to get within challenging distance. The attacker may also dribble out of the side of the grid closest to the goal to win the duel.

The defender must deny crosses and keep the attacker from dribbling out of the grid on the goal side. To win the duel, the defender must take the ball from the attacker and then dribble out of the grid on the side near the ball supply.

Considerations:

• The defender must always position himself to prevent penetration dribbling by the attacker.

- Once he is in line to deny dribbling inside by the attacker, the defender can then start to close the distance to the attacker, aiming to discourage and ultimately deny the cross. There is a fragile balance between being tight enough to prevent crosses and also avoid penetration dribbling by the attacker. Too tight and the attacker will be able to round the defender; too loose, and the cross will be available to the attacker.

- An important point of emphasis for the defender is the idea of preventing outside foot crosses. In most cases, the attacker will be more comfortable crossing with their outside foot as they face goal. Thus, if the defender can focus on turning the attacker away from that foot and onto the inside foot, the defender will be able to limit the effectiveness of the crosser. Inside foot crosses, struck while facing back up the field, generally have in-swinging spin, meaning they will fly toward the goalkeeper as well. Finally, turning the attacker back up the field will also create more time for defenders to filter into the defensive structure in front of goal, and they may be able to step up, creating an offside situation for advanced attackers, and more space for the goalkeeper to pick off crosses.

- Another consideration involves the abilities of both players. A very fast defender can take more chances against a less speedy attacker.

- The defender should learn to use the end line and touchline to his advantage, driving the attacker near one or both of these boundaries to limit the options for the attacker.

- The defender must be careful in defending the end line in particular. Attackers will drive to the end line and try to either gain a cross or force a corner kick if the defender is able to deflect the cross. The defender should learn to turn his body, and particularly his shin guards, back up the field at the end line, both forcing the attacker back up the field and also often deflecting any attempted cross from this position back onto the field, rather than over the end line.

- The defender should learn to sprinkle in fakes to tackle, disrupting the rhythm and planning of the attacker.

- Another tip for the defender in this situation is to tell them to try to mirror the footwork of the attacker. If the attacker takes five steps toward the end line, the defender should match that number, keeping him in line to block a cross and deny penetrating dribbling.

- If the defender can force the attacker to turn his back to the goal to shield the ball, the defender should adopt a more conservative approach as the danger of a cross or penetration dribbling is temporarily diminished. Pressure must still be applied, as the attacker will want to work back into a crossing or dribbling position, but it's important not to foul an attacker at this particular moment.

1V1 DEFEND CROSSES NEAR GOAL

Player 1 drives to the end line and crosses into the area, attempting to pick out the run of the target player (2). The defender (3) and the goalkeeper work together to try to prevent a goal. Play through two touches in the box to both expedite play and ensure all players are actively trying to win rebounds or muffed cross or clear attempts. Rotate roles as desired.

Points of emphasis for the defender and goalkeeper:

- The goalkeeper must communicate regarding her intentions. "Keeper" or "away" should be called early on to help the defender understand her priorities. The goalkeeper is typically tasked with dealing with crosses between the posts and inside the 6-yard box, though some will be more or less aggressive.

- The defender must work to get both the ball and the attacker in her vision as soon as possible. As shown, her first footwork is to establish a goal-side position and then she must close with the attacker.

- If the goalkeeper's call is to pursue the cross, the defender attempts to inhibit the attacker's run to the ball, both throwing off her timing and altering her direction in a way that will prevent her from getting to the cross. Secondarily, if the ball remains loose in the area, she moves to shield the ball for the goalkeeper to cover, to clear the ball or to cover behind the goalkeeper.

- If the call from the goalkeeper is "away," then the defender must either move directly to clear the ball (if she is confident she can get to the ball first) or to inhibit the progress of the attacker to the ball—both wrecking her timing and also trying to change the angle of the attacker's approach, allowing the defender to arrive first and clear, or to interfere with the attacker's attempt to finish. It is important to emphasize that the defender cannot foul the attacker, and that good defenders live in the "gray" area between a foul and no contact with the attacker. The defender cannot hold, trip, or commit other obvious fouls, but if she can get shoulder-ahead to the ball, she can control the attacker's run by slowing her own movement. Failing good positioning, just getting contact with the attacker (for instance when the latter looks to head the ball) can often be enough to alter or take the sting out of the attacker's finishing effort.

1V1 ATTACKER FACING AWAY (1)

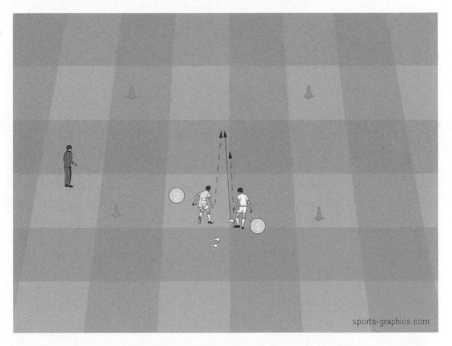

When an attacker has the ball facing away from goal, the defender must use the attacker's limited options to his advantage. This exercise helps defenders recognize and manipulate such situations. The defender (1) passes the ball into the grid, being sure to put the ball into the far half of the area. The attacker (2) runs onto the ball and is given a free first touch, with the condition that this touch must be made facing away from the trailing defender. The attacker tries to dribble out of the bottom of the grid, and if the defender wins the ball, he tries to dribble out of the top of the grid. Play until the ball leaves the area and then change roles and begin again.

It is important to show defenders how to close in this situation. If the defender gets too tight, the attacker can spin off and run out of the bottom of the grid, winning the duel. If the defender allows the attacker too much space, he can turn and face the defender, eliminating the defender's advantage. A useful phrase to teach defenders in this case is to get "touch-close." In other words, the defender should be roughly an arm's length away from the attacker.

1V1 ATTACKER FACING AWAY (2)

sports-graphics.com

This diagram shows the defender establishing proper distance and posture to the attacker shielding the ball. Once he is "touch-close," the defender should adopt a posture that puts his eyes on the side where the ball is with his feet on the other. This position allows the defender both to coax the attacker along and adjust to any change of direction by that player without getting beaten in the duel. The goal here is to force the attacker to try to take a positive touch (i.e., in the direction of his attacking goal) and then tackle before he can face up.

As always, it is useful to remind defenders that, while they must be patient and avoid giving up the advantage, they must still compel the attacker to focus on the ball and the duel and not his options. This is accomplished by a combination of fakes to tackle and physical pressure (use your hands, but do not earn a foul call!).

Jonas Föhrenbach of Heidenheim (right) defends Malik Batmaz from Karlsruhe.
(picture alliance/dpa | Uli Deck)

1V1 ATTACKER FACING AWAY (3)

This diagram shows the defender finding the right moment to tackle. After containing the attacker, the defender waits for the attacker to try and take a positive touch and then moves to separate him from the ball, being careful to make shoulder-to-shoulder contact.

One important detail here is the length of the attacker's touch. If his touch is short, the defender must be careful as the attacker may be able to get the next touch and turn away from the committed defender into open space on the other side. Ideally, the attacker is under enough pressure that he plays a longer first touch, which is a clear signal for the defender to intercede.

1V1 ATTACKER FACING AWAY (4): ATTACKER TRIES TO CREATE SPACE TO TURN

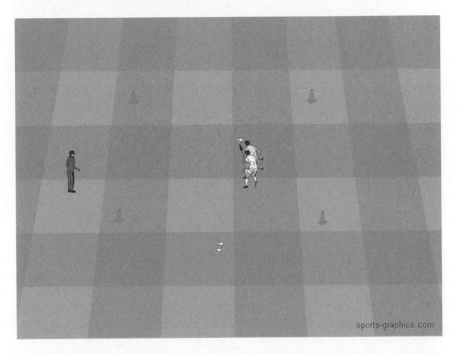

In this situation, the attacker looks to create space to turn and face up with the defender by pushing the ball away from himself with a negative touch. This is a common tactic used by attackers to reset their duel, relieve pressure, and assess their options.

The defender's response must be swift and decisive. While the ball is not at the feet of the attacker, the defender can run right up the attacker's back, applying heavy pressure. Often, this will compel the attacker to pass the ball rather than deal with the relentless defender. Note that if the attacker gets reestablished on the ball, the defender must then get back to a "touch-close" position so that he does not get turned.

1V1 LONG GRID WITH LONG PASS SERVICE

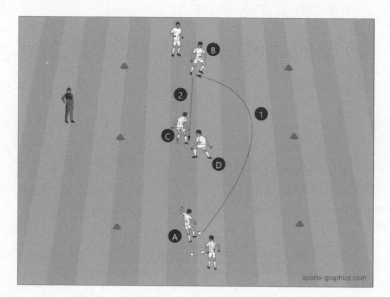

This environment is an example of how the coach can add technical demands to standard environments to challenge advanced players. Player A serves a long pass through the air, over C and D in the middle of the grid, and onto the feet of player B. Player B attempts to play with one touch, setting the ball to player C, who must try to turn the defender and dribble over the end line and the bottom of the grid. If player D wins the ball, he tries to dribble out of the top of the grid. Play continues as long as the ball remains in the grid area. The rotation at the end of the sequence is as follows: A to D, D to B's line, C to A's line, and B to C.

Points of emphasis:

- Technical delivery of the long pass. Can all players produce a quality, consistent pass with either foot?

- Quality "set" or control first touch by the player receiving the long pass.

- The attacker in the middle tries to get faced-up with the defender as soon as possible.

- The defender uses "touch-close" defending and keeps his eyes on one side and his feet on the other to prevent the attacker from turning and to control the latter's movements.

1V1 AIR DUELS: SIDE-BY-SIDE

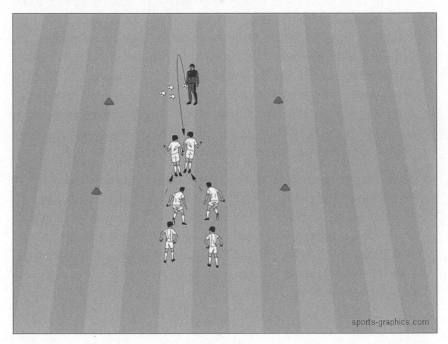

sports-graphics.com

The coach serves balls into the grid (thrown). The players dueling for the ball cannot enter the grid until a signal is given by the coach, just before the serve. Players attempt to head the ball back over the perimeter of the grid on the server's side. The coach should vary the height and length of the serves to challenge the players to get into good defending positions and win the duel.

Coach:

• The priority is to get to the ball first. If the player can get his shoulder out in front of the opponent on a serve that requires forward movement, he will be in good position to win the duel. Conversely, moving forward too quickly will result in defeat if the serve is too high or deep for the charging player. Thus, players must learn to read the flight of the ball and then adjust their position to gain an advantage.

• Another crucial acquired skill in aerial duels is managing contact with the opponent. Players must learn to expect and even initiate contact when the duelers are side-by-side as shown in the diagram. Though contact must be shoulder to shoulder, players are encouraged to get their arms (not elbows) out as sensors to feel the opponent and for balance in the air. Initiating shoulder-to-shoulder contact helps the player manage the influence of the opponent, as unexpected contact can jar the player and ruin their judgement and approach to the ball. By initiating contact, the player can limit the interference from the other player. Conversely, if the player's opponent is first to the ball, it is important to get physical contact with the opponent as a defender in the hope of altering, even slightly, the opponent's trajectory and limiting their ability to play the ball with any force.

• Finally, players must become accustomed to jumping to head the ball. Remaining on the ground will typically not get the player to the ball first. To win the duel, the player must learn to coordinate judging and approach to the ball, getting contact with the opponent when side-by-side, and then jumping high to head the ball. For back-line players, in particular, it is critical that can head the ball over distance from these situations and under immense pressure.

1V1 AERIAL DUELS FRONT AND BACK (1)

Here is a simple environment for teaching players to participate in aerial duels. The coach serves from outside the grid and there are two lines, as shown. There is also a target goal outside the grid and off to the side for the back-side player to try to head into.

AERIAL DUELS FRONT AND BACK (2)

To initiate the duel, the player from the nearest line walks out into the grid. When the ball is tossed, the player from the back side of the grid enters, and both try to win the aerial duel. The staggered starting lines help to create front/ back aerial encounters.

The front player, if he can get to the serve, tries to flick the ball over the defender and on to the next player in the defender's line. The defender wants to head the ball into the small goal outside the grid area.

The approach and jump technique for the defender in this instance is an important training topic, as fouls and injuries, as well as being beaten in the duel, are risk factors. The defender needs to be decisive immediately after the serve. If he cannot get to the attacker before the latter flicks the ball, he may decide to hang back and win the ball after the flick. If he feels he will get to the ball but the attacker will have a definite advantage, he will want to get close to the attacker and even get contact—legally—and then get a very high jump to try to interfere with the flick.

If the serve is high enough and deep enough, the defender approaches with the intent of winning the duel with a strong heading technique.

The defender's approach angle is very important. If he must approach from behind, the defender must try to find an angle that will allow him to get to the ball first but not create head-to-head contact with the attacker. Sometimes this means choosing an angle that is over one shoulder of the attacker, allowing the defender to also get easier, earlier access to the ball.

The defender must be taught to plant one or both feet close to the attacker and then jump up, but not through the attacker.

The defender's arms will often have contact with the attacker, but it is important that the defender develops good habits that do not include using the elbows at all and avoids using the hands to limit or control the jump of the attacker. The temptation is to place a hand on the attacker's shoulder to control him or to propel the defender's jump even higher, but this is a frequently called foul, and in training, the defenders must learn to avoid this tactic.

Bremen's Ömer Toprak (right) defends Hanover's Sebastian Kerk.
(picture alliance/dpa | Daniel Reinhardt)

AERIAL DEFENDING: SERVES, THROW-INS, PUNTS

Young players find aerial dueling for serves, throw-ins, and punts particularly daunting. In addition to concerns about flailing elbows, crashing heads, and awkward landings, young players also need lots of practice to learn how to judge the flight of the ball and also jostle with an opponent for position.

The environment in this drill isolates each of these areas into simple, efficient training drills useful for helping players refine their approach for dealing with aerial dueling situations. In each instance, a server launches balls for a pair of players to try to win. The attackers (in white) are looking to flick the ball over the defender and into the small goal. The defenders want to get the first touch on the ball and preferably powerfully eject the ball from the area, usually with their heads.

Coach:

- The defender must start in a goal-side position.

- The defender must control the physical challenge, initiating and then being able to dominate the space where the ball will arrive.

- The defender must learn to judge the flight of the ball and be able to put himself in position to get the first touch on the ball. In other words, with a lofted ball, he must be able to put himself into position to contact the ball at the highest possible point while also screening the attacker from contact with the ball at any time up to that point. With a lower, driven ball, the defender must be able to establish his body position in front of the attacker and then use either his feet or his head to eject the ball from the area with a single touch.

- The defender needs to be physical without using pushing or pulling, which can both lead to foul calls. Rather, he must be able to use decisive movement and strength to establish position.

- When he jumps, the defender needs to go straight up, not launch himself into the attacker. Additionally, whether jumping from one foot or two, he must learn to keep his arms at his side, with the hands and elbows slightly extended to control space and provide cushioning balance, but not flailing at the attacker or anywhere near the ball, which can lead to a handball.

- As with all dueling situations, much of success is determined by mentality. It's important not to think in terms of violence and aggression but rather of being dominant in the space and controlling variables such as position and timing.

1V1 DEFEND THROW-IN (1)

sports-graphics.com

Defending throw-ins is a situational tactical requirement often overlooked in training, but given the frequency of throw-ins in the match, this is an important coaching consideration. Player 1 throws the ball in for the attacker (2) to try to win. Player 2 aims to dribble over the end line of the defender (3). Player 3 must defend his end line and try to win the ball and dribble over the attacker's end line on the right in the diagram.

The defender must remain goal side of the attacker until the throw is released and then can only move to get in front of the attacker if the defender is absolutely certain of winning the ball and the duel. If this calculation is wrong, the defender loses the duel and his team may lose on match day due to his recklessness.

If the attacker gets the first touch on the ball, the defender must move to try to prevent the attacker from facing up toward the defender's goal. This entails getting "touch-tight" to the attacker, applying pressure without allowing himself to be immediately turned. Much depends on the first touch of the attacker. If the attacker plays the ball up in the air and/or in a negative direction with his first touch, the defender must move while the ball is in the air to either win the ball or apply immense pressure to the attacker to force a subsequent poor, or at least negative, touch.

Another common tactical concern is the use of "dummy" runs by the attacker(s). Many teams will run a player back toward the thrower to try to draw in the defender and then throw the ball over the defender's head. Coach players to understand this danger and help them understand that a less-contested throw in front of them is better than any throw behind the defender. In other words, if necessary, on match day, hand off the runner to another defender or concede the short throw to be able to defend the more dangerous space behind.

1V1 DEFEND THROW-IN (2)

This is another frequent development in throw-in situations. The thrower (1) tosses the ball down the touchline and the attacker (2) and the defender (3) give chase. Note that in the diagram, the defender's first move is to cut out the run of the attacker by moving between the attacker and the ball.

Once established between the attacker and the ball, the defender is confronted with a difficult dilemma in that he is up against the line and facing his own goal. In this situation, a confident defender may try to dribble to beat the attacker, but it is useful to encourage players to consider a more conservative option. Many defenders will turn and knock the ball off the attacker's outside shin, earning a throw-in and resetting the tactical situation to his team's advantage. One means of incorporating this option in the exercise is to add the rule that the defender can win the ball by earning a throw or dribbling over the attacker's end line.

DEFENDING FOOTWORK: RECOGNIZE 1V2

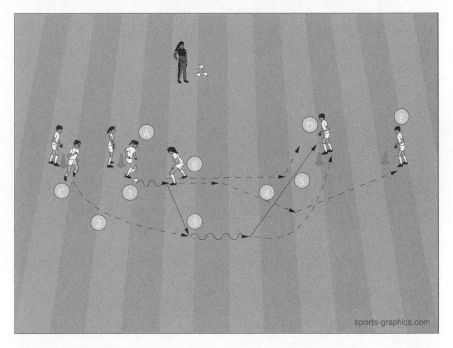

This warm-up uses a simple overlap to teach players to recognize an evolving 1v2 situation, and conditions them to respond by backing off and keeping the play in front of them. Player A dribbles (1) at the defender (player B). Player B defends as if she is dueling with player A only. Player C makes an overlapping run (2), creating a 2v1 situation. Player A passes to player C. Player B, the defender, backs off, jockeying to stay goal side and between the two attackers. Player C takes several dribbling touches, then passes to player D, and the sequence repeats in the other direction.

The rotation pattern is as follows:

- Player A becomes the defender in the next sequence.

- Player B joins the overlapping line (E).

- Player C joins the attacker line (D).

FC Union Berlin defend in front of goal.
(picture alliance/dpa | Andreas Gora)

1V2 BUMPER (1)

This exercise is an excellent way to introduce and tune players' ability to recognize and defend 1v2 situations. The defender (1) passes in to the attacker (2) and moves to close down. The attacker has the option to try to beat the defender on his own or to use the bumper (3), who is limited to one touch and can only move up and down along the side of the grid, as shown. Both the defender and the attacker aim to win the ball and dribble over their opponent's end line. Rotate roles and positions after every duel.

The defender must first learn to recognize the danger of the added attacker. The restrictions on the movement of the bumper at this stage make it easier to highlight and control the dilemmas facing the defender.

Most young defenders will be beaten by a 1-2 between the attacker and the bumper as soon as the defender commits to closing down the attacker. The first lesson is that the defender should do all he can to control variables and that he should serve the ball away from the bumper side of the grid and then close down by taking away the pass to the bumper.

1V2 BUMPER (2)

In this drill, the defender has closed down with an arced run designed to take away the pass to the bumper. Once this is accomplished, the defender must try to maintain the separation between the attacker and the bumper while simultaneously ratcheting up the pressure on the attacker. This is a delicate operation that requires repetition to understand the shading of emphasis and attention between the man on the ball and the support player.

Observe:

*   Most inexperienced defenders, having been beaten by a 1-2, will go too far in their efforts to cut off the pass to the bumper and will then be defeated by an attacker who simply dribbles past them. Defenders must cut the pass angle to the bumper (note that the bumper will learn to move down the perimeter to try to create a passing angle) while also preventing dribbling penetration.

- If the defender can isolate the attacker, he should try to win the duel in the space where he has contained the ball and the attacker. In other words, he must not reduce his pressure and must maintain the isolation of the attacker. If, for instance, he relaxes and allows the attacker to turn back and connect with the bumper, the defender will likely lose the duel, despite starting well.

1V2 BUMPER (3)

- Defenders will also learn that if the pass to the bumper is made (A), they must immediately back off (B), keeping the attacker in front of them, and allowing themselves a chance to intercept the return pass (C). Note that the defender must learn to be able to keep both the ball and the runner in his vision. Many defenders will turn away from the ball to chase the attacker, diminishing their ability to participate in collective, tactical defending in addition to making it easier for the bumper and the attacker to connect on the return pass.

1V UNKNOWN

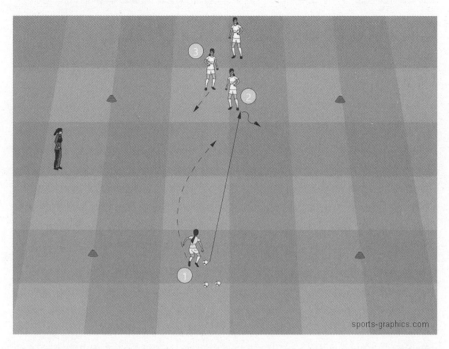

The defender (1) serves to the attacker (2) and closes down. The next attacker in line (3) can join at any time to create 1v2, or she can let the 1v1 play out. The defender must gauge her approach and movements to account for the possibility of an extra attacker arriving at any time.

In addition to learning to account for another possible attacker, the defender in this exercise will want to try to separate the attacker from potential support—another useful tactic—and she will have to think carefully about when to tackle and trying to catch the attacker off-balance, i.e., after a poor touch.

There is a tendency among attackers to slow the pace here and just wait for another attacker to help them. It is advisable, to keep training intense and realistic, to limit the length of the duels (10–15 seconds) and if the ball is still in the grid when time expires, the defender wins.

If the defender does win the ball, she tries to dribble over her opponent's end line. The attackers try to dribble over the defender's end line. Rotate the defender after each duel.

SECOND DEFENDERS: COVER AND DOUBLE

As players work to understand all aspects of individual defending, they must also learn the advantages of combing their defending into groups that allow for more complex, layered defending. The most basic combination of defending blocks is that of two players. The player nearest the ball is the *first* defender, responsible for pressuring the player on the ball and also for making play predictable by influencing the attacker through movement and intimidation.

The *second* defender provides cover for the first defender. The most critical aspects of this role are the positioning and communication of the second defender. The covering defender(s) will generally position themselves under (goal side) and adjacent to the first defender, off one shoulder. The distance between the players will vary, but a useful visual is to think in terms of each of the players holding one end of a corner flag post. The second defender must be close enough to cut off the run of the attacker if the first defender is beaten. The communication of the second defender with the first defender is made in short, sharp statements of direction: "Left!" or "Right!" designed to both let the first defender know that she has cover and also that she should drive the attacker in the direction of that support.

Teaching second defender roles can be very challenging. Players tend to grasp the concept well in isolated, grid-fixed exercises, and then much of the recognition and communication in particular, tends to dissipate in the run of the game. That said, it's important that coaches continue to demand attention to the covering role, as any defensive structure will need clearly understood covering roles to be successful.

SECOND DEFENDER: MOVEMENT AND COMMUNICATION (1)

Players A and B work together to demonstrate first and second defender roles and also the interchanging of those roles. A and B approach the two attackers from the lines (C, D) at the bottom edge of the area. The possession players pass the ball back and forth while remaining at their respective cones. Importantly, the attackers hold the ball each time until the defenders have set their defending positions.

In the diagram, player A closes down the attacker on the ball, getting between her and the goal (which is only there for demonstration at this time), and she also orients herself to force the ball back toward her helping player (B). Player A also calls "Ball!" indicating recognition of her role as the first defender.

Player B is shown in the second defender role, able to cover player A if the latter were beaten on the dribble while also being in position to get to the other attacker as the ball moves. A useful visual for this situation is to have A and B each hold on to one end of a corner flag to highlight approximate spacing. Player B also calls sharply to her partner "Right!" indicating the direction of her support to player A.

When the ball is passed from one attacker to the other, the defenders interchange roles as shown. Player B calls "Ball!" and moves, as shown, to both pressure the attacker on the right and force the ball back toward her helping player (A). Player A moves to the second defender role, getting underneath her partner to provide cover, while also calling "Left!" to help orient her partner's defending.

Each defending pair should complete six role interchanges, then the defending pair takes the place of the attacking pair and a new defending pair (C, D) enters the area.

This is an ideal environment, with the ability to stop and control the action and quiz the players about their priorities, their placement, movement, and communication.

SECOND DEFENDER: MOVEMENT AND COMMUNICATION (2)

In this progression, the attackers are allowed to try to pass the ball into the small target goal if they feel the defenders are not denying them the angle to the goal. The idea here is to both provide urgency for the defenders in their movement and to give them an understanding that their deployment within the defensive concept is meant to shut out passing angles to more advanced attackers and to the goal itself. In the example, players A and B shift roles with the movement of the ball and the receiving attacker decides to test player B's ability to screen the goal. Player B's movement, however, is correct (note that she is cutting the angle before closing down—an important detail), and she cuts out the pass.

SECOND DEFENDER: TEAM WARM-UP (1)

This is a useful means of reinforcing first and second defender roles, footwork, and communication in a team setting. In each triangle (1–4), two attackers pass a ball along the perimeter of the area. Simultaneously, two defenders work inside the triangle, setting first and second defender roles each time the ball moves. Use the central flag as a goal for the defenders to orient themselves in their movement and choice of angles. Emphasize quick, coordinated movement and communication. Require the attackers to hold the ball until the defenders are set before passing to their partner. Play for 40 seconds, then change roles.

SECOND DEFENDER: TEAM WARM-UP (2)

In this progression, at the signal from the coach, one defender in each triangle moves clockwise to the next triangle. In the diagram, the players move at the signal. Another simpler means of identifying which players move would be to designate one player in every grid to move with each restart.

The point of the progression is to remind players that the environment is always changing, and they will constantly have to identify and reset their roles and supporting teammates.

The coach can further complicate the environment as follows:

- Players move clockwise or counter-clockwise, depending on the signal (i.e., "A" or "B").

- Players move directly to the opposite side of the grid, creating more traffic to sort out at the center area.

- Give all players a designation (i.e., "1" or "2"), with a 1 and a 2 in each grid. If the coach calls "1!" all the 1s move. If he calls "2!" the 2s move.

Finally, the coach can combine calls, i.e., "2, A" to indicate that the 2s move clockwise, etc.

SECOND DEFENDER: DOUBLE-TEAM (1)

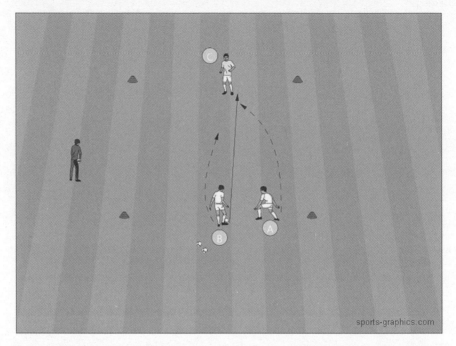

One of the important permutations of identifying and executing the second defender role is the ability to set double-team opportunities. In this exercise, two defenders (A, B) serve to a single attacker (C), who tries to dribble past both defenders through the bottom of the grid. Notice that A closes down immediately, forcing C to dribble to the direction of his defensive support in player B.

SECOND DEFENDER: DOUBLE-TEAM (2)

In this follow-up drill, the two defenders recognize that the single attacker has no support options. As A pressures C, B joins A in stopping the attacker's run and seizing the ball. It's very important to emphasize that there is danger in this situation because if C is able to split A and B with his dribble, for instance, both will be beaten. Therefore, the players do not arrive at the same time, and the first player in is tasked with stopping or at least slowing the attacker's run and also forcing his eyes down through pressure. If B sees both of these conditions met, he can then join the duel. This staggering of positions and roles helps to limit the danger of penetrating runs by the attacker that could beat both defenders. Needless to say, communication and understanding between the defenders is also critical to creating and executing the double-team.

Leverkusen's Florian Wirtz (middle) is double-teamed by Freiburg's Lukas Kübler (left) and Kevin Schade.
(picture alliance/dpa | Philipp von Ditfurth)

SECOND DEFENDER: 2V2 IN A GRID (1)

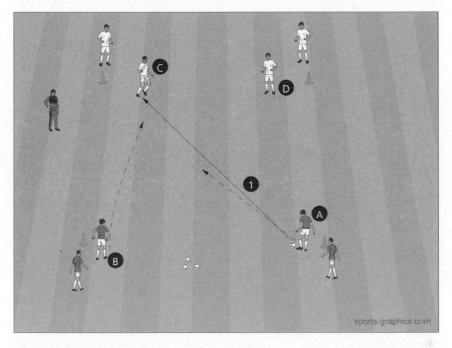

Playing 2v2 in a grid to end lines is a simple way to introduce and refine second defender behavior. Players A and B duel against C and D. A passes to either opponent to initiate the duel. In this case, player B will call "Ball!" and close down C as he receives. Note that B is angling his approach to coax the attacker and the ball to his right, where his covering defender (A) will be. A duly moves to support B, adopting a covering position that allows him to deal with a dribbling threat from C (should he beat B) and also contain attacking activity by D.

Both teams try to dribble over their opponents' end line. Play until the ball leaves the area and then the resting players initiate the next sequence. This environment lends itself well to quick stops by the coach to adjust player movements and positioning.

SECOND DEFENDER: 2V2 IN A GRID (2)

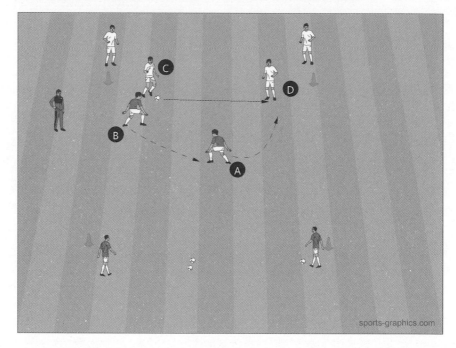

This drill highlights the standard exchange of roles between defenders as the ball moves and allows players to perform these movements, with the associated communication, with active opponents. As C passes to D, A calls "Ball!" and moves to contain and pressure D, showing the ball and the player back toward his arriving cover in player B. As B moves to a supporting position, he calls "Left!" affirming to A that he is arriving to cover.

For young and inexperienced players, it is useful to require one to two stationary passes between attackers at the beginning of each sequence so that the defenders have the opportunity to rehearse this basic movement before play goes live.

SECOND DEFENDER: 2V2 IN A GRID—PREVENTING 1–2 COMBINATIONS (A)

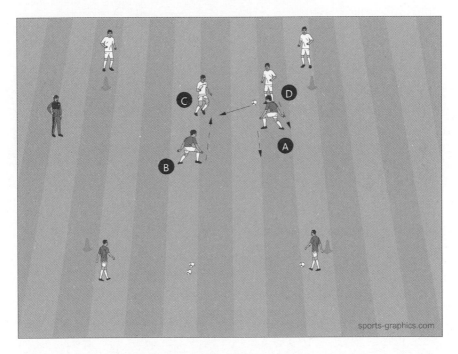

One of the more difficult problems that arise for players as they learn cooperative defensive roles is the prevention of combination play by the attackers. In the diagram, player C is moving to a position where he can play a 1–2 with D, thereby playing out defender A. Coaches need to spend time demonstrating this danger to players and then showing potential responses.

In this example, the defenders opt to push B—the second defender—higher to either intercept the pass to C or at least block the possibility of the return portion of the combination to D, who is going to try to get behind A. Note that A senses the danger as well and backs off, keeping D in front of him and adopting a covering position to B's advanced location.

SECOND DEFENDER: 2V2 IN A GRID— PREVENTING 1–2 COMBINATIONS (B)

Here the defenders demonstrate another effective response to the attackers' efforts to execute a 1–2 to play A out of the defending picture. In this case, A recognizes the danger of C's approach and moves to cut out the angle of the potential pass, isolating D on the ball. In response to A's movement, B slides to his right, maintaining covering depth but giving himself a better support angle.

It is worth noting that similar solutions are viable for tracking and dealing with overlapping runs as the first defender can shift his control angle to force the first attacker away from the runner, and the second defender can maintain his depth while adjusting his angle of support to absorb the runner's presence while covering the first defender.

SECOND DEFENDER: EMPHASIS 4V2 RONDO (1)

Rondo small group possession exercises are often used to imprint first and second defender roles. Indeed, these can be very useful, with the caveat that because play is not directional, the transfer of the training element to the game is not always immediate, particularly with young players.

4v2 in a 10 x 10-yard grid is a nice environment for the coach to examine the players' ability to grasp the first and second defender roles through their movement, communication, and interchange.

From the outset, the defenders must learn to quickly define and change roles. In the diagram, the defender nearest the ball steps decisively to cut off the pass to her uncovered (left, as she looks at it) side, and then closes toward the ball. She knows to do this because her partner calls "Right, right!" to let her know where her support is located. Note also that the covering defender begins to move to an assisting position underneath the first defender and off her shoulder.

SECOND DEFENDER: EMPHASIS 4V2 RONDO (2)

This diagram shows the importance of corralling the ball in a defensible area when the defenders are outnumbered. When the desired pass is made, the covering defender moves to isolate the ball and not allow the attackers to release pressure by playing behind the defenders; her movement to the right cuts out that crucial pass. Meanwhile, the other defender moves to a covering position, behind and off the shoulder of the first defender.

SECOND DEFENDER: EMPHASIS 4V2 RONDO (3)

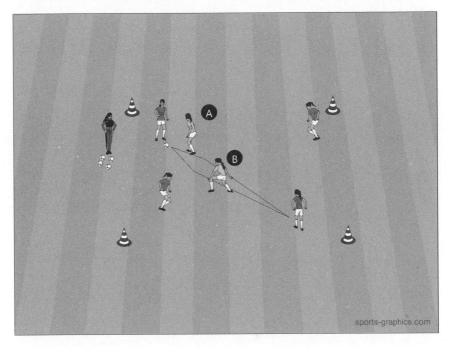

Here we see the subtle calculations involved in the placement of the second defender. The diamond represents the window through which the attacker would like to play to her teammate, defeating the pressure of the two defenders and playing them out with a single pass. Player B cuts this pass out through her positioning while also preparing to pressure or cut out the pass to her left. Thus, the defenders work to isolate the ball and then ratchet up the pressure on the attackers with their movements until they force a mistake or can challenge a single, isolated attacker for the ball.

If the defenders win the ball, they play to the coach at the edge of the grid. Rapid restarts from the coach at the edge of the grid keep the game intense for the players, and it's important to change out the defenders after 1 minute to emphasize the importance of quick, determined movement by the defending pair.

SECOND DEFENDER: EMPHASIS 4V2 RONDO: HIGH PRESSURE

sports-graphics.com

In this variation, waiting pairs of defenders serve a ball into the area for the attackers and then enter the area, determined to use high pressure and first and second defender tactics to win the ball from the attackers. As soon as the defenders win the ball or knock it out of the area, they run out, and the next pair of defenders pass a ball to the attackers and play resumes. This practice serves a number of purposes, from more intensive training of defending roles as play is very fast to rewarding defenders for winning the ball quickly as they then get to rest. Similarly, the attackers learn that if they move the ball well, they can wear down the defenders and have a bit more rhythm and success in their efforts to keep the ball.

2V2+4: SECOND DEFENDER EMPHASIS

Perhaps the best small-sided environment for teaching the role of the second defender is a simple setup that allows for efficient role identification and transition. Players A–D place two players in the grid (A, B) and two players at the cones at the bottom of the grid (C, D). Team E–H place two active players in the grid (E, F) and two players at the cones at the top corners of the grid (G, H). The coach has a supply of balls and is ready to initiate restarts when the ball leaves the grid.

Players A and B play against E and F. Players A and B try to pass the ball to C and D, who must remain at the target cones. Players E and F try to pass the ball to G and H, who must remain at their target cones.

Note that teams try to play to targets in their team color, but receive the ball from the other team's target players. For example, after A passes to D for a point, D then looks to pass to E or F to restart play. This restriction is often confusing for younger players early on, and walking through this pattern helps clarify player roles.

Additional rules:

- End-line targets cannot play to each other, on the same end, or target to target. This restriction keeps the focus on playing in the grid rather than easy passes among target players.

- End-line players cannot be tackled, but must limit themselves to two touches and 5 seconds in possession to keep play flowing along.

- Attackers can play back to target players from the other team. This rule allows the attackers to relieve pressure and keep possession while forcing the defenders to problem solve with each reset.

- Rotate the active pairings every 2 minutes.

Another important coaching nugget to help make this an efficient training environment is to emphasize to the attackers in the grid that they need to move up and down in the grid and interchange positions when looking to receive the ball from the opposing targets to initiate play. Otherwise, play can become very stagnant.

2V2+4: SECOND DEFENDER INTERCHANGE

This diagram shows the movement of the two defenders with the transfer of the ball from one attacker to the other. As A passes to B, F moves to become the first defender and force B to look back toward A. E simultaneously gets underneath F's position as the new second defender. Emphasize communication with each transfer of the ball, with F calling out "Ball!" and F calling out "Left, left!" indicating that he is moving to a covering position and that he wants F to show the ball back toward A.

An often overlooked coaching point in this scenario is the importance of each player getting visual confirmation that their partner is with them and moving to the new position. In other words, as F moves to close down B, he must sneak a quick look to ensure that E is moving to support him. To illustrate this point, stop the exercise and tell E to sit down where he is. Ask F how this would affect his positioning. Point out that if the player's partner falls down or misreads the situation, the player would have to play in a considerably different, conservative fashion. He would certainly back off and try to keep play in front of him. Thus, it must become habitual for players to check their support with each movement of the ball.

2V2+4: SECOND DEFENDER SCREENING THROUGH PASS

Another critical teaching point highlighted by this scenario is the necessary consideration by the defenders for the possibility of a through pass. As E and F move, they must cut out the through pass by B to either C or D, which would immediately defeat their collective defending position. The coach should use a quick freeze to point out that the defenders must assess the possibility of a through pass by an attacker and adjust their pressure and cover angles to cut out any such pass.

2V2+4: SECOND DEFENDER PREVENTING COMBINATIONS BY ATTACKERS

A final consideration for the defenders is the importance of coordinated defending against combinations that would defeat their defending position. In the example, the attackers (A, B) prepare to execute a 1–2 to get B in behind F and likely earn a point by passing to targets C or D.

There are three potential responses for E and F to this dilemma:

- Player F could back off, keeping both attackers in front of him. The concern then would be that there is no pressure on B, who might be able to find C or D with a through pass.

- Alternatively, F could alter his angle of pressure (1), getting into the passing lane and separating B from A. If this becomes the designated response, E must then change his support angle, moving sharply to his right and F must be taught to continue to apply pressure to B and deny any notion by the attacker to dribble forward.

- A third response would be for E to close down on A in such a way as to either deny the pass from B to A or cut out any angle for A to play back to B. If this response is chosen, it must be noted that the defensive pair will lose defensive depth, and F must move to become a second defender, getting under E.

What is clear from this discussion is that adjustments to deny 1–2 play by attackers necessitate clear planning, rehearsal, and communication among defenders, as confusion and defeat will meet any improvisational or hesitant response.

It should be noted that other combinations, from overlapping runs to heel passes, designed to upset defending postures must be dissected and schemed against for the defending concept to be successful.

SECOND DEFENDER: 1V2 18-YARD BOX (1)

The defender roles for confronting attackers near the goal need careful instruction and rehearsal. Here the coach passes to the lone attacker (A) near the top of the 18-yard box. Two defenders start from a marker at the penalty spot. The attacker must take at least three touches before shooting. Play until the ball leaves the area, a goal is scored, or the goalkeeper wins possession of the ball.

The two defenders must first decide who among them will be the first defender. Here B takes the initiative and closes down the attacker at the top of the area. Player C moves to a covering position. Verbal communication must be decisive, with the first defender calling the ball and the second defender indicating her presence and angle of support.

Because of the danger of a shot at goal, the defenders' behaviors need to be tweaked to try to prevent the attacker from penetrating or trying to finish. The first defender, while trying to steer the attacker to her right and her support, should also get tighter to the attacker (2 yards and closing when feasible). After initially steering the attacker, the defender must also adopt a more square posture to block any shot attempt. This tighter, open position is more at risk of being beaten on the dribble, but some risk is necessary to try to discourage and block shots.

SECOND DEFENDER: 1V2 18-YARD BOX (2)

This diagram demonstrates the importance of the two defenders adopting squared-up, tighter positions when there is a danger of a shot at goal. Player C, the first defender is close enough to steer the attacker to her support on the right side. Player B, the second defender, works off the shoulder of the first defender and is tighter to her partner than she would be in other areas of the field. The first defender should try to match the steps and footwork of the attacker, looking to block any shot attempt and trying to force the defender to face away from the goal or dribble to an angle of decreasing danger and parallel (not closer) to the goal. The second defender moves along, also tightening her distance as the danger increases.

In some circumstances (i.e., if the attacker is able to get out ahead of the first defender with her run), the two defenders may need to change roles. In that event, B would step hard to the ball and C would drop off her left shoulder and try to accelerate across behind B to her right shoulder, completing the switch. This is not an easy transition, but the emphasis here is keeping a broad blocking presence in front of the attacker.

SECOND DEFENDER: 1V2 18-YARD BOX, ATTACKER FACING AWAY

sports-graphics.com

This is a variation of the previous exercise that demonstrates an important variable in the defenders' response to an attacker receiving in the area. In this case, the attacker receives facing away from goal. Because this player cannot shoot without facing up, the first defender, while being careful not to allow the attacker to post up and spin past her, can get tighter and apply more pressure than in the open field, as the defenders must take the initiative to fluster and dispossess the attacker. Similarly, the second defender, while staying in a covering position, should move to support her partner off the most threatened shoulder. In other words, the second defender matches the orientation of the first attacker's shoulders as she tries to turn and then remains off the first defender's shoulder and within 2 yards of her partner, helping expand the width of the defending block in case of a shot attempt and also looking to win any long touch forward by the attacker.

SECOND DEFENDER EMPHASIS: 2V2 18-YARD BOX

This exercise complicates the defending picture for the defenders by adding a second attacker. The coach passes a ball into the "D" for the attackers to retrieve. While A runs onto the ball, B opts to overlap.

The defenders, C and D, begin from a marker at the penalty spot. In this instance, D becomes the first defender, approaching the ball at a slight angle to encourage the attacker to steer toward the second defender's (C) covering position. In this way, C and D manage to absorb the runner off the ball (B), while focusing on the danger from the primary attacker (A). The next diagram shows an alternative approach for the defending group.

Play until the ball leaves the area, a goal is scored, or the goalkeeper gains possession.

SECOND DEFENDER EMPHASIS: 2V2 18-YARD BOX—ALTERNATIVE DEFENDING APPROACH

sports-graphics.com

This is the same setup as previous drill. In this instance, the first defender, C, opts to force the ball in the other direction and her partner covers on her right as the arrows indicate.

This approach has the advantage of isolating the first attacker, A, from her partner, B. The catch however is that B has now eluded the defensive structure created by C and D, and if A can find a way to pass to B, the defenders will not be able to recover in time to prevent a penetrating run and shot at goal by B.

The point, then, is that coaches and players must carefully consider the implications of angles of approach and support, particularly when defending near goal, as some strategies may appear to offer distinct advantages to the defending group but also may pose more risk.

SECOND DEFENDER: DENY CROSS (1)

Ideally, back-line players become well-versed in denying crosses, and an important element in thwarting crossing efforts is getting a second defender involved. Defender A passes to winger B to initiate the sequence. Player C, the nearside center back, observes A closing down B and opts to join and cover A, approaching on the goal side of A and in position to block a driven cross, cover A if B dribbles past him, influence B to not cross or perhaps turn back up the field, and potentially double-team the attacker if the situation warrants.

Target D works on timing his runs to goal and tries to finish any cross that is played into the area. The other center back (E) and the goalkeeper defend in the area. If a ball is crossed into the 18-yard box, player C must recover and try to join the defending group. Play in the area until a goal is scored, the goalkeeper gains possession, or the ball leaves the area. On the flank, if the ball is played away or controlled by the defender(s), the play ends, and the next group of players starts a new sequence.

The playing relationship between the wide back and the nearside center back is the focus of the exercise. Player C, the center back, must communicate his intentions clearly and often to his teammate, and the two must swap roles in some cases. For example, if the ball is pushed behind A to the end line and C opts to intervene, A must recover toward the end line and cover C in case B is able to win the ball and threaten the goal.

The center back must judge each situation carefully, as the tighter his coverage of the wide back, the greater the gap between himself and the other center back in a match situation. If the wide back is an accomplished dueler who has shown the ability to dominate this particular runner, the center back may opt to remain a bit more central and let his teammate control the situation. If, conversely, the winger is a dangerous, explosive player, the center back will need to judge each incursion to decide when it's best to intervene. If the wide player can stymie the original run (i.e., stop or turn back the attacker), then the center back will have better options. Statistically, very few goals are scored from crosses near the touchline. The wide back and center back can often combine their efforts to pressure an attacker into facing away from goal and forcing him toward the touchline, and being well-versed in first and second defender roles is critical to shutting down the attacker's options and pushing him to the line.

SECOND DEFENDER: DENY CROSS (2)

This diagram shows the development of the play with the center back (C) in the second defender role, covering the defender (A) on the end-line side. Note that this positioning is likely to discourage the attacker (B) in his aspirations to round A and to the end line. Again, the balancing variable here is the subsequent threat to the area between the two center backs (C, E), which can be threatened if the attacker turns sharply back up-field and finds an onrushing teammate. The individual characteristics and experience of the defenders, as well as the designs for the defending group put forward by the coach, will influence just how aggressive the center back should be in supporting the wide back.

SECOND DEFENDER: DOUBLE-TEAM (1)

The second defender role can be used to create double-team situations within the defensive construct.

Double-teams require:

- Presence of multiple members of the defending team near the ball.

- Communication regarding roles and desired steering of the attacker.

- Marking or shadowing of all close passing options available to the attacker.

- Timing to ensure that the attacker is unable to find an exit option.

- The first defender must contain the run of the attacker and make that player focus on protecting the ball (eyes down).

- The second defender must arrive while the attacker is preoccupied with the aggressive movement of the first defender.

- The two defenders must cooperate to ensure the attacker is not allowed to escape the double-team.

In the example, the right back (B) has been beaten down the touchline by the attacker (A). The center back (C) prepares to step in to stop A's progress down the line. The right back will double-team A, closing down from an up-field position.

In this case, although a defender has been beaten on the dribble, the second covering defender is in good position to step in and become the first defender, while the recovering player now becomes the second defender.

It's also worth noting here that areas along the touchline are ideal for double-teaming because the defenders can use the line to further limit the options available to the attacker to defeat their pressure.

SECOND DEFENDER: DOUBLE-TEAM (2)

This second example of a double-team situation involves a common occurrence along the flank. The attacker (A) has been corralled along the touchline by the right back (B). B's pressure has stopped A's dribbling run and turned him to face the touchline. Note the clear limiting of passing options available to the attacker as well as the presence of the center back (C), who covers B, allowing the latter to play with more aggression. This situation allows the recovering winger to close down on the ball, joining B to double-team A.

SECOND DEFENDER: DOUBLE-TEAM (3)

This final example of a double-teaming opportunity shows the potential for closing down attackers between the lines in the defending structure. Attacker A has been turned back on her dribble by the pressure of the center back (B), who has stepped out of the back line to confront her. The holding midfielder (C) recognizes that A will have few options given the number and positioning of defenders in the area, turns, and doubles down on the attacker. Note that her run angle is very important in this situation as she is approaching A along the attacker's best path for a pass to defeat the pressure. Thus C must approach quickly and in a way that the outlet pass does not become available.

Double-teams in central areas are more difficult to execute given the many ways for the attackers to dribble or pass out of pressure, but even unsuccessful efforts disrupt the rhythm of the attackers and may lead to passes or dribbling that result in eventual loss of possession for the attackers.

A final note—this example also highlights the need for defending teams to close their horizontal lines. Attackers are increasingly adept at exploiting the soft areas between defensive lines, and the larger these spaces become, the more attackers will find spaces in there to show and receive. If the lines become stretched, any efforts at double-teaming will require longer runs to close down attackers, allowing more time and space for the attackers to defeat the pressure.

SECOND DEFENDER: 4V4 GAME TO DOUBLE-TEAM

Small-sided games can be used to help players recognize and execute double-team opportunities. The diagram features a 4v4 game. Each team attempts to dribble over their opponents' end line. The coach conducts restarts from the touch area to keep the game moving at a fast pace.

Try to help players recognize both the implications and moments to double-team. In this situation, player E has dribbled into the center of the grid, where A has stepped in and turned E back toward her own end line. Because C has taken away a pass to an opponent through close marking (while remaining in a covering position for A), and because the angle of pressure from A is driving E away from F, her best support pass, B must recognize that she has the opportunity to double-down on the E. B must, however, understand that her movement must continue to deny a support pass to her immediate opponent (angles indicated through solid lines). Thus, B's approach must include awareness of her immediate opponent's movements (she must look as she moves), and her angle must be adjusted to continue to take away this pass.

It's important to note that there is still a chance that E will be able to play to F, defeating the pressure and double-team. However, the defenders must understand both that they must try and try again until they succeed, and that if the pass to F is made, the defending team is still in very good position, with all their players behind the ball and the most advanced opponents well-marked.

SECOND DEFENDER: 5V5 TO CORNER GOALS— DOUBLE-TEAM EMPHASIS

sports-graphics.com

This is a 5v5 game to four corner goals. Each team defends the goals on one end line and tries to score in their opponents' two goals on the other end line. The coach conducts restarts from the touchline, as shown.

Because the goals are in the corners of the area, there will be much play along the touchlines and thus ample opportunities for the coach to identify and teach double-teaming moments. In the diagram, player E dribbles near the touchline, trying to reach the goal at the top of the area. Defender A has moved to cut off the direct route to the goal. Note that his approach blocks the pass to the goal and also steers the dribbler to the touchline. This angle severely limits the options for the attacker. As A approaches, C and D tighten their marking of their nearest opponent, recognizing that these two are the best relief options for the attacker. Then player B steps away from his nearest opponent and to the ball, closing down with an eye toward helping pin the attacker to the touchline and also discouraging him from looking or playing back toward his own goal. Once again, the angles and timing of the approach are critical to successful double-teaming. If B approaches too early or late, he may leave E an opportunity to play out of pressure and compromise the defensive structure. For similar reasons, A must apply continuous pressure on E, keeping the attacker's head down, limiting his ability to see his options as the defense tightens around him.

As a side note here, coaches need to continually emphasize that it's important to look for and take advantage of double-teaming opportunities. Youth players have a natural instinct to want to assume that if a player is confronted and they are off the ball, they should remain with their mark or in their space and let things play out. Thus coaches need to say often that it's ok, even preferable to go ahead and swamp an attacker with multiple defenders, so long as the defensive structure is not compromised through the double-teaming action.

SECOND DEFENDER: 4V4 IN THE AREA—DOUBLE-TEAM EMPHASIS

sports-graphics.com

Two teams of four play to score goals inside the 18-yard box. Restarts come from the coach, who is posted at the top of the "D." Note the two resting players, one from each team, located 30 yards from goal. If the defending team wins the ball, they can play to this resting outlet player. That player is then allowed one free pass to near the top of the area, signaling the change in role (offense/defense) for each team.

The defending team, as part of their effort to stymie the attackers, should look for chances to double-team an attacker in possession. In the diagram, attacker C is dribbling across the face of the goal, attempting to improve his shooting angle. Defender A has stepped up to pressure C, but is unable to turn him back outside to decrease his shooting angle. Defender B has no direct mark at the moment and recognizes the danger of a shot from C, so he steps up, double-teaming C with A. Note that his presence also effectively doubles the width

(B+A, shoulder to shoulder) of the block that the defenders create in front of goal and discourages a shot.

The coach should "freeze" the action several times to show when a double-team is feasible, emphasizing that the wider the shooting angle available to the attacker, the more important it is to double-team.

This is also an important moment to show players that one of the critical components of double-teaming is that the movement of the second defender does not compromise the defensive structure of the group or team. This is a similar situation to that portrayed in the previous diagram. However, attacker E is in a much more dangerous position between defenders and ahead of the ball. Player B, as the second defender, is also starting from a slightly deeper position, meaning he has farther to cover to achieve a double-team. In this situation, B's run should be to a position to block a pass to E, while still supporting A's defending against C. A double-team may be possible as the situation develops, but the coach must point out that these subtle differences dramatically affect the ability of the group to double-team the attacker.

THIRD DEFENDERS: GROUP BALANCE

The final element in the basic tactical teaching of defending is the role of third defenders. In general terms, these field players are all the team members not close enough to the ball at that particular moment to serve as either first or second defenders. Traditionally, this is a bit of a nebulous teaching topic for coaches, as few popular training exercises highlight the role of a third defender, and there is a tendency to simply refer in passing to third defenders as players off the ball who provide *balance*.

To be sure, balance is a critical component of defending. Players off the ball must ensure that the entire defensive structure is not compromised by failure to provide early and ongoing depth, awareness, communication, and an organized response to potential threats. Those in the third defender role often also provide important outlets for building unpressured possession as the team transition.

One of the themes of this book is that with the growing speed and sophistication on the attacking side of the ball, the ability of defenders to adopt and swap defending roles at speed will be necessary for teams to blunt attacking initiatives successfully. In other words, meet increasing speed and organization with more speed and organization. To do this, defending structures need players who can anticipate the need to tighten defensive groups and players who aggressively recognize and execute all three tactical defending roles so that pressing, zonal defending, lines of confrontation and restraint, and more can be collectively executed with efficiency and consistency.

THIRD DEFENDER: 8V8 FOUR-ZONE GAME (1)

This game helps players easily understand some of the critical roles third defenders play, as well as the rapid change of tactical defensive roles. Some of the third defender responsibilities highlighted in this environment are balancing, screening, anticipation, and marking.

Divide the group into two teams of eight players and place four players from each team in zones, as shown, with each group isolated from their teammates by a group of the other team in the zone in between. The coach serves balls anywhere in the area for restarts. The two teams try to keep possession in their zones, and they must try to play the ball to their teammates in the other zone as often as possible. The defending team can send two players into an opponent zone when the ball is in that area. If the ball is in an end zone, both defenders come from the adjacent zone. If the ball is in one of the central zones, one opponent must enter from each of the two adjacent zones. Otherwise, players are confined to their zones. The coach should rotate the team's groups between end and central zones, so that players experience the game from both positions.

THIRD DEFENDER: 8V8 FOUR-ZONE GAME (2)

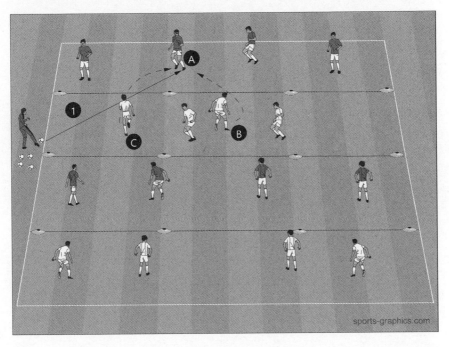

THIRD DEFENDER: 8V8 FOUR-ZONE GAME (3)

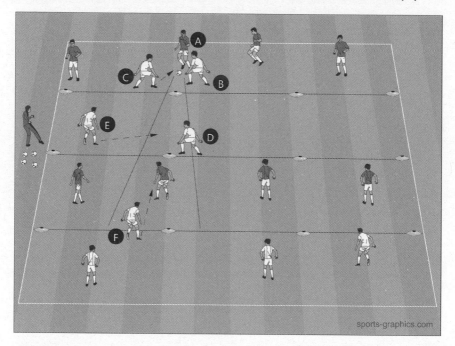

This diagram emphasizes third defender roles in this scenario. While B and C have adopted the first and second defender roles and are moving to squeeze and double-team A on the ball, D and E are moving to screen passes through the only forward angles to A's teammates in their central grid. A useful teaching point here is to tell D and E to place themselves on the inside shoulder of the defender in front of them (B and C), as that cue will help them find the right angles from which to screen.

An often overlooked opportunity to help players off the ball engage is to point out that the players in the bottom grid, seemingly uninvolved, should be preparing to move to win any ball played from the far grid into the area adjacent to their own portion of the grid. For example, player F has recognized that he should get to the edge of his grid and be ready to sprint in to win any ball that eludes the defenders and screeners in the two active lanes of the area. Similarly, D's position at the back of his own grid gives him the best chance to pick off a through ball and leaves him very close to the opponent's target grid, so he too can move quickly to confront any successful change of grid.

THIRD DEFENDER: 8V8 FOUR-ZONE GAME (4)

In this final example, player A has successfully lofted the ball over the defending group to his teammate B. Defenders C and D move to execute the first and second defender roles. Players E and F are sliding across as third defenders, preparing to screen the most likely passing angles for through balls back to the zone where A is located. Note that G is also taking the initiative to move to the edge of his grid with the thought that he could jump in if C and D are unsuccessful in closing down B and the latter passes to teammates near G. Note that under the rules of this game, D would have to recover to his own zone for G to become an active defender. G and his teammates are providing defensive balance in the sense that they can prepare for a number of eventualities, making the defense more in-depth and flexible, just as the team must be in a regular game.

As an aside, there are numerous variations to this game that can further highlight the third defender roles. For example, the coach can require that all switches of zone must be through the air *and* any defenders can enter the target zone as soon as the ball is in the air. This restriction creates an incentive for players off the ball (third defenders) to recognize and act early on changes in the game that bring the ball close to them.

THIRD DEFENDER: ZONE GAME (1)

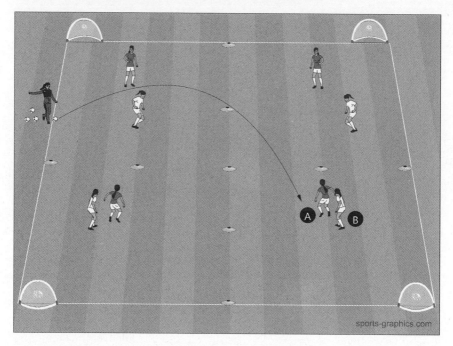

This game again uses zone restrictions to help players identify third defender roles, adopt early the posture and actions required of third defenders, and help them recognize that third defenders still play an active role in the game.

The teams play 4v4 to four corner goals. Each team defends two goals on one end line and attacks the other two goals on their opponents' end line. All restarts come from the coach along the touchline.

In the opening phase, all players are restricted to their respective zones, with one player from each team in the four zones, as shown in the diagram.

The isolation of the players into their respective grids will often create a fairly stagnant game. It's important to note that a brief period of this type of ball-watching highlights the way players off the ball can sometimes view the game; the coach must then get to work identifying how both teams should behave in the off-ball zones.

THIRD DEFENDER: ZONE GAME (2)

This drill is a good starting point for helping players understand that actions in all four zones will influence the game. Player A has received the ball and B has moved to close her down, keeping A facing her own goal.

Because A appears to need assistance, her two teammates in their defensive half are moving to support positions. Players C and D of the defending team must anticipate this movement and work to cut off the angles to any support pass, isolating A from negative passes to relieve pressure. Players C and D are performing important third defender roles that allow B to play more aggressively in defending A.

In the attackers' other forward zone, player F has adopted a nearly square support position to A, perhaps looking to set a 1–2 to get A free of B. Player F, who now has both second and third defender responsibilities, has taken up a position to pressure F and perhaps interfere with a combination with A. However, E has to balance her defending to prevent F turning up-field and beating her to the goal in the corner of their area. That danger forces her to limit her aggression with regard to F and shade her positioning to contain F near the cone line if she receives the ball.

THIRD DEFENDER: ZONE GAME (3)

In this picture, the speed at which roles can change is highlighted. Player B has just won the ball from A. Immediately, C and D now become targets as they check to the ball in support of B, who is pressured by A. Simultaneously, the opponents in their zones now have to defend, and they become third defenders, attempting to cut off angles of support to B. However, C's marker has come too tight to her, and C spins off and runs into space to receive the forward pass from B. E, meanwhile, has moved into a supporting position underneath B in case she needs to turn the ball back to avoid A. F, who, moments ago, was contemplating a combination with A, has now become a second defender, getting underneath A.

This drill emphasizes the relevance of player roles off the ball through all phases (attacking, defending, transition) and also how important it is for players to transition between phases with all possible speed in support of their teammates.

THIRD DEFENDER: ZONE GAME (4)

In this example, the coach has changed the rules to allow one additional attacker and the opponent defending that player to enter the grid where the ball is in play.

Player C has control of the ball and her defender has moved to pressure her and deny her access to the near goal. B has entered the grid and started an overlapping run. Player A, who should be a third defender—as shown in the previous iterations—now has a problem. She has been slow to recognize that her opponent may enter the play, and her recovery run does not allow her to mark B. Player C passes to B, who scores in the open corner goal.

The situation depicted here is a frequent occurrence in the full game. The attackers expend much energy and run themselves deep into their opponents' end and find themselves out of position when the ball is lost and their immediate opponent decides to join the attack.

The lesson here for A and her teammates is that while sometimes they will be caught out of position in transition, they must immediately think that, as third defenders, they should at least begin their recovery run when the ball is lost so that their immediate opponent is not so wide open, and their early run may discourage the use of the overlapping run, leaving attacker C with fewer options.

The other defenders in the diagram have all performed third defender roles. Player F is goal side of E and sits at an angle to cut off support passes to that area. Player D's opponent remains underneath D and in a position to cover her defending partner and block the corner goal if needed.

DEFENDING FROM THE FRONT: TACTICAL CONSIDERATIONS FOR FRONT-LINE PLAYERS

Front-line players are critical to the defending mission of the team. These players form "the tip of the spear," as they are often the first to apply pressure to and steer opponents in possession, particularly when the ball is lost in the attacking half of the field, and if they are successful in winning the ball, they can put the team back on the attack very near the opponent's goal.

The recent emphasis on team pressing has highlighted the role of the forward line in defending, as these players are required to do a lot of running in large, open spaces, often without immediate reward, to lead the team's press. Thus, fitness and work rate, as well as perseverance, are critical to the makeup of effective front-line defending.

Another important consideration is the number of players deployed along the front line. Almost all teams put one, two, or three players along the front line, and the team's approach to front-line defending will be heavily influenced by this choice. This variable has become much more complex in recent years with the blurring of formation designations. Twenty years ago, teams were typically defined very clearly as 1-4-4-2 (two forwards) or 1-4-3-3 (three forwards), etc. More recently, many 1-4-3-3s have been further refined to be considered 1-4-2-3-1, or similar derivatives. Many teams play one formation in attack and then deploy a different layout when defending. The point here is that with the reduced reliance on rigidly defined formations, coaches have had to rethink and blend defensive tactical planning to fit their particular vision for their team, and for that reason, tactical discussions like this one will be broad in nature, highlighting concepts and principals for coaches to comb in, tweak, or discard as their team planning evolves.

DEFENDING WITH THREE FORWARDS
FORWARD DEFENDING: CENTER FORWARD (1)

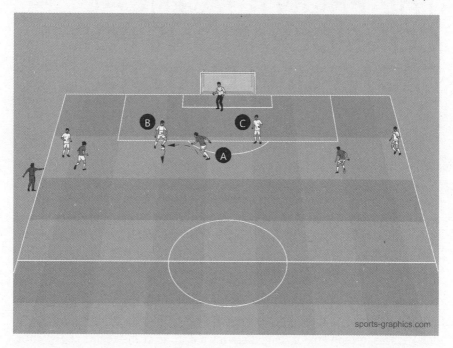

In a three-front, the center forward is chiefly responsible for pressuring and splitting the two center backs in possession. In the diagram, the center forward (A) uses a curved run to split the opposing center backs (B, C) and then close down B on the ball.

While it is not universally true, most teams do not want their center backs dribbling out of the back because of the concerns in case of a turnover and/ or because these players often are not playmakers accustomed to running the ball forward under pressure. Therefore, it is often the design of the defending strategy to use the forward players to try to compel the center back to hold the ball and try to dribble out of pressure, hoping for a turnover.

FORWARD DEFENDING: CENTER FORWARD (2)

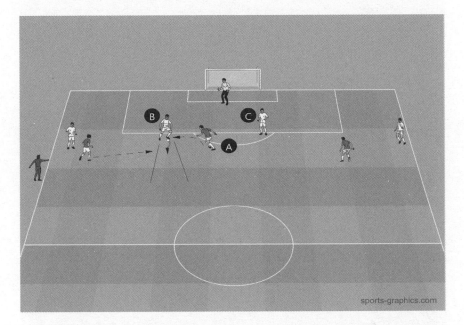

This picture continues the sequence showing the center forward (A) closing down one center back (B). Here the wide forward recognizes that the pressure from A is forcing B to dribble forward, and he pushes inside as well, helping steer B forward. This action, "pinching," creates a funnel, shown with lines on the field, wherein the players in the midfield and on the back line can see the limited passing angles available to B and begin to take away those options through screening and marking. It's important to note that when forwards close down, they must continue to monitor and close out passing angles to the other backs and, where possible, to the goalkeeper as well.

FORWARD DEFENDING: CENTER FORWARD (3)

Another defending role for a center forward in a three-front involves double-teaming a holding midfielder under pressure. In the diagram, holding midfield A is under heavy pressure from midfield B, who has the attacker taking a negative touch and turning away to face his own goal. Center forward C recognizes this situation and looks for a moment to double-down on A. As C moves toward A, he must try to block at least one of the passes to the two center backs (D, E) that would release A from the pressure being applied. This effort is often in vain, as the opponent has multiple outlet passes available. However, in making the effort, C and B have made A uncomfortable, which he will remember, and they may force a mistake from the opponent in this possession or in the future. Also, the fact that the midfielder has been forced to turn back will allow the defending team to push up and keep the opponent further from dangerous areas near the goal.

sports-graphics.com

Center forwards are also tasked with pressuring the opposing goalkeeper in possession. This is a daunting proposition, as it sometimes leaves the forward isolated and chasing the ball between the two center backs and the goalkeeper, particularly now that goalkeepers are expected to be able to play comfortably with their feet.

However, the center forward's pressure has a number of potential outcomes that merit his full efforts. First, as the diagram shows, the center forward's (A) approach to the ball can begin to limit the goalkeeper's choices. The solid lines indicate the reduced angles of play available to the goalkeeper. This view also helps his teammates anticipate the next pass and mark accordingly. The center forward's priorities are to win the ball if possible or force a long or errant pass that can lead to a turnover. Alternatively, if he can force a pass to the wide back near the corner, that pass, particularly against a three-front, can be a trigger for the rest of the team to press and force the opponent to try to claw their way out of a difficult situation. Finally, center forwards learn with experience to first take away the pass to one center back and then, if they can get close enough to limit the goalkeeper's ability to see the field, also make it difficult to find the other center back. Then the goalkeeper may freeze a bit, allowing the center forward to win the ball, or the goalkeeper may just spray the ball away to break the pressure.

Center strikers must also be prepared to make an extra run to force the goalkeeper to pick up the ball when the latter decides to drain away time with a lead. The need to act in this regard and make the runs early and with resolve preserves time for the team to try to battle back in the match.

Again, it is very important to emphasize to front-line players that the pressure schemes will not always create an immediate result but that their efforts are necessary as part of the defending philosophy and will bear fruit through determined, repeated effort.

FORWARD DEFENDING: WINGERS (1)

At first blush, the wingers in a three-front have fairly simple defensive responsibilities. These players must prevent their opposing wide backs from influencing play. Where possible, the wingers need to deny service to the wide back and win duels against that player. If that player gets forward, the winger must track the run (see next diagram).

Particularly at a time where high, early pressing is popular, the contest between the wingers and the wide backs has evolved to include some subtle, if very important, considerations. In the above diagram, A has allowed enough space for the goalkeeper to consider it safe to throw the ball out to the right back (B). Once the goalkeeper has committed to throwing to B, A can then close down immediately, and she should try to turn B back toward her own end line with tight pressure. Note that A can either pin B to the line with a curved, inside approach or force her back toward the center of the field, where her supporting teammates will organize to try to win the ball. The coach must decide, based on the team's overall defending philosophy, whether the wingers should immediately mark the outside backs and force longer distribution or, if the team would prefer the ball be played short, then the wingers can learn to tempt the pass to the wide back and use that as a cue to initiate the press. Alternatively, though not common in a formation featuring a three-front, some coaches choose to set a line of confrontation further up the field (i.e., at the top of the circle), which would see the entire front line withdraw—when the ball is lost or the goalkeeper is in possession—to the line of confrontation.

FORWARD DEFENDING: WINGERS (2)

Wingers must also, as previously mentioned, track back if the opposing outside back on their side of the field opts to join in the attack. In the diagram, opposing winger A has driven to the end line where she is confronting the outside back. Opposing outside back B decides to join in the attack and goes forward to look for a support pass from A. Winger C must track this run and get goal side of the outside back. If she cannot deny the pass to B, she must prevent penetration dribbling or service to the front of the goal by driving the attacker to face the touchline or her own goal.

Wingers often find chasing the opposing back to be onerous duty, and they are often late to recognize the need to make the defensive run. However, it is important that they understand that, in some situations, there may not be a way to absorb the run of the opposing back if the winger cannot get there, and that the defensive structure on that flank will be outnumbered and likely compromised without her run.

FORWARD DEFENDING: TWO STRIKERS

FORWARD DEFENDING: TWO STRIKERS DEFENDING WIDE (1)

If the team deploys two strikers, the defending strategies for the front line are quite different. In this diagram, the opposing center back has passed the ball wide to the outside back (C). The nearside striker for the defending team (A) sprints to apply pressure to C. B, meanwhile, adopts a middle position, prepared to pressure back-passes to the center back or the goalkeeper, but also to retreat toward the center line, depending on the result of A's pressuring of C (see next two diagrams).

FORWARD DEFENDING: TWO STRIKERS DEFENDING WIDE (2)

In this continuation of the previous diagram's action, player A, the nearside forward, has succeeded in turning the outside back (C) toward his own end line. This is the ideal outcome as it denies penetration running or passing by C and severely limits his options in possession. Reading this development, B, the other striker, can now push further forward, anticipating a back-pass from C to either the center back or the goalkeeper.

FORWARD DEFENDING: TWO STRIKERS DEFENDING WIDE (3)

In this instance, the nearside forward (A) has failed to turn back the wide defender (C), and the latter begins a dribbling run up the touchline. In this case, A must continue his run, if possible catching and turning or dispossessing C, and at least pressuring him into releasing the ball forward in the relatively limited angle spread shown. Although not an ideal outcome, A's efforts allow the rest of the team to at least anticipate and prepare for a pass into this area. Players D, E, and F can all tighten their marking or drop to cut out a through pass as appropriate. It is noteworthy that A's run allows both F and D to remain in deeper and more central positions, respectively, because they do not have to move to stop a deep dribbling run by C.

Note that the second striker once again reads the angle of pressure and arrival at the ball by A to help him sort out his own run. In this case, because C is dribbling forward, there is no reason for B to remain in an advanced position, and he can thus drop into a position more connected to the midfield defending group, as shown. From here, he can pick off or pressure passes to the opposing defensive midfielder.

Strikers playing in two-fronts often ask when and how far they should track a wide player running forward. The answer will vary based on the abilities of the players involved and the designs of the defending group. However, in general, the wide forward should track and pressure wide players running forward if they can close the distance successfully, especially in the attacking half of the field. Most defending units will detail a wide midfielder or an outside back to deal with the runner in the back half of the field. However, mobile, active strikers often double-down on a wide back in those circumstances or move, at a minimum, to cut out back-passes.

FORWARD DEFENDING: TWO STRIKERS DEFENDING CENTRALLY (1)

In most cases, two forwards defending against the ball in a central position will try to encourage the opponents to keep the ball in a central position. In this example, right center back C has the ball in his own 18-yard box. Striker A moves to pressure him. Note that A's run is a curved affair, strongly discouraging C from playing to his outside back. The other striker, B, moves laterally to his right first, threatening to intercept any pass from C to the left outside back. Then, as A coaxes C back to a central orientation and pressures him a bit, B and start to cheat toward D, the other center back. In this way, A and B form a funnel through which they want C and D to play. Ideally, the midfield and back-line players, as shown, use this cue to mark players in their areas more tightly, tempting C to try to dribble out of trouble. By definition, most center backs are not very comfortable running the ball under pressure, and mistakes and turnovers can be expected.

Note that in most systems of defending, the forwards are expected to continue to track and pressure a center back dribbling into the attack. Often, a midfielder will be able to step forward and, while screening out any pass to a player they were marking, close and stop a dribbling run by a center back. Again, the tracking striker will be expected to participate in the closing down, pressing the dribbler toward the center of the field and forward. If the striker fails to maintain an outside position on the center back, the latter will be able to pass the ball to his outside back teammate, and the defensive structure will be momentarily compromised. Indeed, the greatest challenge of defending with two forwards is persevering when most of the efforts, particularly in the front third, will be defeated by the opponents. Players must understand that they are outnumbered in this area, and that their work is designed to wear down and ruin the confidence of the defenders in possession and also help limit the options the attackers have in developing their possession.

FORWARD DEFENDING: SINGLE STRIKER

FORWARD DEFENDING: SINGLE-STRIKER SYSTEMS (1)

It is increasingly less common for teams to play with a single striker, though some still do against vastly superior opponents or with a lead to put more players behind the ball. In this example, the defending team are configured as a 1-4-5-1 or, if you like, a 1-4-4-1-1. Regardless, the point man is a lonely character, playing 1v4 or worse if the goalkeeper is involved. In these circumstances, the team usually plays a lower line of confrontation, often near the top of the circle.

In the diagram, the lone striker, player A, remains tight to the defending block until the opponent's center back, B, approaches the top of the circle. At that moment, B makes a curled run that steers the man in possession toward the narrow side of the field. In essence, this is the critical task of the single central striker: divide the opposition, pushing their attack to one side of the field, and then try to help keep the ball on that side.

FORWARD DEFENDING: SINGLE-STRIKER SYSTEMS (2)

In this continuation of the previous action, one can see the limits of the single striker in defending in wide areas.

The defenders' response is as follows: Right midfielder D leaves his immediate opponent and steps forward to stop the dribbler. Right back E moves up and to the right to cover D and also takes away any pass to the opposing outside midfielder. The remaining three backs slide across, and the wide midfielder on the back side drops down to maintain the length and width of the back line.

For the purposes of the current topic, the most important notation here is that, unlike in a two- or three-forward system, the single forward does not chase opponents in wide spaces. First, he likely cannot get there to apply much pressure, and if the opponents manage to reverse the ball, he will be upward of 70 yards from the ball. He must stay in the central area to continue to discourage the opponents from reversing fields along their back line.

The lone forward's presence in the central channel is also absolutely critical in transition. Because the team have placed four players in the back line and five in the midfield line and then closed those lines to defend tightly, their shape when the ball is won will not be ideal for maintaining possession. The lone forward acts as a "hanger," dwelling in that center channel and between the opponent's back and midfield lines—a central target for outlet passes to spring counterattacks.

DEFENDING IN THE MID-FIELD: THE IMPORTANCE OF MOBILITY AND FLEXIBILITY

Perhaps the most complex considerations for the coach regarding defending are schemes to defend in the midfield. Like the front line, much depends on the number of players deployed and the posture of the midfield group. As systems of play have blurred in recent years, even the number of players along this line is open to much debate as some will insist that their 1-4-2-3-1 uses five midfielders, while someone watching the same group will be certain they are looking at a 1-4-3-3, and that the players in question are wingers along a three-person front line. Indeed, just changing from attack to defense will typically influence the layout of the team, and a team may attack as a 1-4-3-3, but defend as more of a 1-4-5-1, or some variation. In the end, the interpretations matter less than making sure that the scheme accords coherent emphasis along all lines, and it's also important to remember that every scheme is an evolving idea that will require tweaking with each new opponent, injury, or even substitution.

Critical points of emphasis for the midfield defending group include:

- The number of players must be sufficient to deal with the large spaces across the midfield.

- The mix of players must include strong ball-winners (air and ground) and more finesse-oriented, speedy, and technical players.

- The mix of players must also be complimentary: they must play well *together*. One player lacking effort or ignoring the team plan will compromise the midfield defending group.

- The design of the midfield group must allow for rapid, successful transition both to defense and attack.

- This group must serve as the defensive engine for the team, providing cover for both the front and back lines, constantly moving to pressure any ball as necessary and forcing the opponent to respect their defensive grit and transitional speed and creativity.

- This group must win a psychological battle against the opposing midfield, in particular, through domination of the space on both sides of the ball.

- The defending group must show tactical flexibility, adjusting their actions to maximize the team's effectiveness against a particular opponent and also to suit the game conditions. For instance, a midfield line will most often behave very differently late in the match when the team is leading rather than trailing.

DEFENDING IN THE MIDFIELD: STANDARD THREE-PERSON MIDFIELD (1)

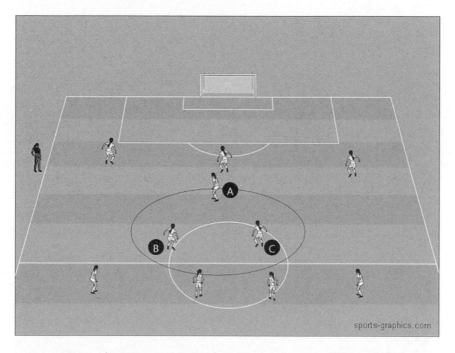

For simplicity and clarity, this study will focus on 3-, 4-, and 5–player midfield arrangements and the most important considerations. The diagram shows a common midfield scheme today, with a pair of defensive midfielders (B, C) and an attacking midfielder in front (A). This arrangement is common to both the 1-4-3-3 and derivative formations (i.e., 1-4-2-3-1). The strengths of this setup include its concentration of players in the center of the field and the presence of two defensive players in front of the center backs, which creates a block in that area that is very difficult to break down. Against a 1-4-4-2 with a flat midfield, the central midfielders enjoy a numerical advantage. Finally, the triangle can be "flipped" to provide more pressure higher up the field, as well as support for the front three in the attack.

DEFENDING IN THE MIDFIELD: STANDARD THREE-PERSON MIDFIELD (2)—AREAS OF CONCERN

The most difficult defending challenge in a three-person midfield configuration is along the flanks. Opponents will typically use this space to organize counterattacks and break pressure. Most teams allow one or two of the triangle players to surge to the flank to deal with these threats (along with a winger dropping down and/or the wide back pushing up), but any movement to the edge stretches and weakens the triangle. As a consequence, the midfielders must be very mobile and disciplined about recovering or, preferably, maintaining their central block.

The other problem area is one that is a concern in all systems of defending. The space in front of the center backs is an area where opposing center forwards lurk, hoping to pull center backs out of position. Coaches at every level expend much energy imploring their defensive midfielder(s) to stay in the area and screen that space so that the integrity of the back line remains undisturbed.

To be sure, this is easier to do with two defensive midfielders, but in some ways, the very presence of two players with split duties (step out, hold) means that there may be moments when the team is caught with one or both defensive midfielders away from this critical space, and the opponents have room to play into their center forward and tear apart the defensive structure.

DEFENDING IN THE MIDFIELD: STANDARD THREE-PERSON MIDFIELD (3)—PRINCIPAL ACTIONS

The diagram demonstrates some of the basic defending functions performed by three central midfielders. Defensive midfielders B and C are screening in front of the center backs and also marking opponents near them as they sense the ball will soon be played into the area. Note that both players are working on the outside shoulders of their respective opponents so that they can pressure this player if she receives toward the center of the field and their defensive concentration, and away from the open space on the flank.

Attacking midfielder A works with the center forward to try to isolate the center back on the ball (D) and tempt that player to dribble forward. Note that A's movement must also screen out passes to the opposing holding midfielder.

DEFENDING IN THE MIDFIELD: STANDARD THREE-PERSON MIDFIELD (4)—AGAINST WITHDRAWN MIDFIELDER

Often the opposition will either play two holding midfielders or one attacking midfielder will drop off, as F has here. This situation requires careful consideration if the team intends to play with two defensive midfielders near the back line. Player B first notes that center back D is being pressured by center forward E. She must also be certain that her partner, C, is in position to protect the space in front of the center backs. Then B slides to her left so that as F receives, she is tempted to dribble toward the center of the field as shown. Then B moves to stop F's run. By delaying her move to close down, B has maintained a position closer to her own back line, meaning that the defending block still has six players along the back line and in the critical space just in front of the back line.

Other important defensive movements here include the tracking of the opposition's right back as she runs up the field by the left forward, and the screening movements by the attacking midfielder (A) to try to keep the ball on the same side of the field. Note that A is then able to help pressure F if she can continue to screen out a pass to her immediate opponent as she closes. She must look as she moves and constantly adjust her angle accordingly.

Some teams will respond differently to this situation, most notably by freeing B to mark F from the outset. Marking people of course has the advantage of clarifying responsibilities and, in theory, maintaining pressure. However, this approach also tends to wreck a team's defending shape (what if C's opponent drops off? Does C chase and leave the space in front of the center backs unprotected?), and it complicates transition, leaving the team in unfamiliar positions when the ball is won.

Whatever the approach, it is mandatory that the midfielders be clear about and disciplined in carrying out their responsibilities. Equally importantly, the overall scheme must take into account the numerous questions that will be asked of the defense and the planned responses.

DEFENDING IN THE MIDFIELD: STANDARD THREE-PERSON MIDFIELD (5)—AGAINST WIDE PENETRATION BY MIDFIELDER

This diagram shows how a defending team, and particularly a midfield three, can deal with a wide penetrating run by an opposing midfielder. The left-side defensive midfielder has stepped out to stop the penetrating run by the opponent. Note that C, her partner, has remained central and now moves to an inside position on her opponent, with the idea of sealing the ball into the half of the field where it is now. Similarly, the attacking midfielder (A), moves to mark the opposing defensive midfielder, and she does so at an angle designed to pin her opponent to the side of the field where the ball is now located. The back line slides across, as shown, and the left winger recovers to cut out passes to the opposing right back. The general philosophy here is that if the team must send B from her defensive midfield perch to deal with a flank incursion, the team moves to contain the penetration to that side and tightens up marking and space to contain the opponents' attack.

DEFENDING IN THE MIDFIELD: FLIPPED TRIANGLE GENERAL CONSIDERATIONS

Some teams, particularly when they anticipate dictating the game to an opponent, will invert the midfield triangle, playing with two attacking midfielders (or one plus a box-to-box player who will push high when the team is in possession) and a single defensive midfielder. Although many of the defending considerations remain the same (for instance, the team will most often still force the ball to the middle of the field where their numbers are concentrated), there are notable differences that it is important to take a moment to consider.

On the plus side, playing two attacking midfielders (A, B) allows the team to have another player involved in pressing the opponent, creating a group of five players who can swamp an opposing back line and midfield group. The added player up high makes a significant impact in tightening the angles for defending immediately behind the front line and means that two holding midfielders for the opponent can be man-marked out of possession, often ruining their ability to control the rhythm of the game. Relatedly, any ball won by this group will likely be captured in an advanced position and with good supporting numbers for counterattacking.

The defensive concerns for an inverted triangle are highlighted in the diagram. First, because the team features a single holding or defensive midfielder, that player is most often required to screen in front of the center backs, meaning that he or she has very limited ability to defend in the gaping holes (1, 2) on either side of the midfield group. The result is often that one of the attacking midfielders or the winger on the side of the ball is repeatedly dragged back to create sufficient support for defending in those areas. Over the course of the match, this requirement can create fatigue and a sagging triangle if the team has to do a lot of deep defending.

Another common issue in this configuration is the central space between the attacking midfielders (3). If the opponent can get a player in that space in possession, it can create issues of responsibility for the triangle. This is a bit ironic given that the team are set up to steer the ball into this space, but a player in this space can run at the defensive midfielder and then feed supporting runs wide to continually tear apart the defending triangle. If the holding midfielder is forced to step forward to confront an attacker, the space behind him opens up, and the team has to contemplate compromising the back four's integrity by pushing a center back in to track a checking forward, and so on.

In addition to making players aware of these potential threats and rehearsing responses that include quick reactions and determined defending by the wide attackers and defenders to deal with the threats to the edges of the midfield, another helpful tool is to teach the midfielders to work off the shoulders of the players at the next level up the field. In the previous example, the attacking midfielder B works off the inside shoulder of the right forward, while the defensive midfielder C works off B's inside shoulder. This cue gives the players the knowledge of where their defensive support will be located and, critically, serves as a constant reminder to the midfield group, in particular, that they must work to tighten their defending shape, as the shorter, consistent lines of their shape will make it harder for opponents to find room to play through their space.

FOUR-PERSON MIDFIELD GROUPINGS
DEFENDING IN THE MIDFIELD: FOUR PLAYERS, FLAT CONFIGURATION: AREAS OF CONCERN

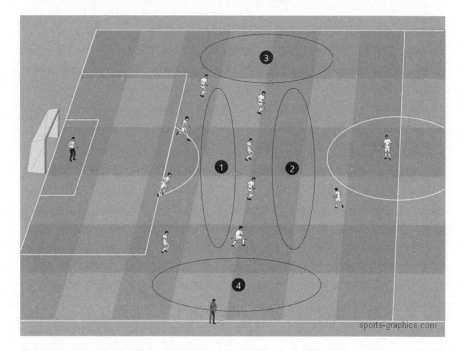

For much of the decade of the 1990s, 1-4-4-2 formations were very popular, and this system still has many proponents. The most commonly cited reasons for the popularity of the 4-4-2, particularly on the defensive side of the ball, include the simplicity of the layout, with each player having fairly straightforward areas to patrol, and also the creation of two mutually supportive blocks of four players, which make the system very hard to break down. Indeed, from Arrigo Sacchi's Italian National Team (1994 World Cup Finalists) down through Diego Simeone's Atlético Madrid, teams that deploy 4-4-2 formations tend to be very strong on defense.

Although the four-person midfield continues to enjoy much popularity, there are limitations and concerns associated with the flat midfield configuration, and it's useful to talk about short-comings as a prelude to how players are usually coached to play. The most common critique of the flat four-person midfield is that unless the team is playing with three on the back line, there will be only two players on the front line. In the era of pressing, it's difficult to get consistent, successful pressure on the defensive side of the ball with only two front-runners. Relatedly, teams playing out of the 1-4-4-2 tend to be counterattacking oriented, forcing opponents to attack the thick block of eight players on the back two lines and then bursting forward when possession is won. This is a fine way to play, but teams playing in 4-4-2s are thus often seen as primarily defensive and likely to concede much of the front half of the field to their opponents rather than playing with an aggressive press.

The areas of specific concern to a flat four in the midfield include the space immediately in front of and behind the midfield line (1, 2) and also the wide areas (3, 4), particularly on the side away from the ball as it's necessary to shorten the line to shrink passing lanes to the opponent, leaving more space on the back side to exploit. The area in front of the defense and behind the midfield is particularly important as a pass to an opponent in that area immediately bypasses the entire midfield line. The area in front is less concerning, except that an unpressured opponent in that area can take time to carve up the defense with any number of passes if the defending block is not disciplined.

DEFENDING IN THE MIDFIELD: FOUR PLAYERS, FLAT CONFIGURATION: BALL OUT WIDE

To create a lively, tight block of defending players, the flat midfield is typically configured into a zonal defending posture. As the diagram indicates, the midfield line is never really flat. The manipulation of players forward and back, as well as the constant tightening of horizontal space, serve to create a shifting, mutually supportive, and challenging obstacle for the attackers to try to solve.

In the diagram, the ball is near the right midfielder (A), who has stepped forward to steer the ball inside toward the rest of the defending block. If the ball is very near to the touchline, some teams will go ahead and force the ball to the line, severely limiting the space and options for the attacker. While the wide midfielder (A) adopts the first defender role, the inside midfielder B moves to a covering position behind and off the shoulder of A. B's mission is to help stop dribble penetration behind A and also to tighten the space between the back and midfield lines, where dangerous passes are likely to be attempted. The other inside midfielder (C) is in a balancing role, sliding to support B and setting the depth of the line. This latter responsibility is especially important as C's position allows him to see both B and A and also to be seen by D, so he is the player to set the depth of the defensive midfield line. If the ball were on the other side of the field, B would adopt this role. In central areas, it is the inside player furthest from the ball. Again, the depth of the midfield line must be calibrated to allow the back line to stay tight to the midfield, but also high enough to get adequate pressure on the ball, particularly in the defending third. Finally, the wide midfielder away from the ball (D) is also in a balancing position, connecting with the outside back to protect the otherwise open space on the side away from the ball.

DEFENDING IN THE MIDFIELD: FOUR PLAYERS, FLAT CONFIGURATION: BALL CENTRAL

This diagram shows the midfield response to a ball near the midfield line in a central position. B is now the first defender and he has stepped forward to apply pressure. Note that as both A and C are in covering positions as second defenders, the ball can be steered in either direction, depending on the team's preferences and the match situation. C is now setting the depth of the line. Player D remains in a balancing position, though he has tightened the distance between himself and C as that space is now under more immediate threat with the ball in a more central position.

DEFENDING IN THE MIDFIELD: FOUR PLAYERS, DIAMOND CONFIGURATION: AREAS OF CONCERN

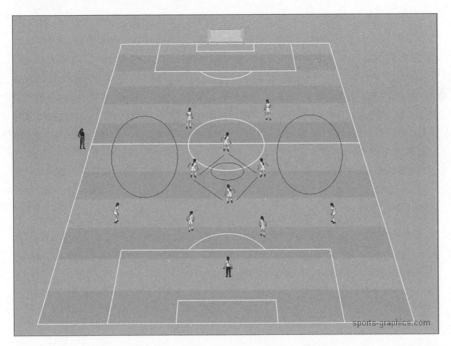

A less popular, but nonetheless interesting variation on the four-person midfield is the diamond configuration. Shown in the diagram, the system deploys a single defensive midfielder, two tucked-in wide players, and an attacking midfielder at the top of the diamond. The strength of this system is readily apparent, as opponents trying to work through the center of the field will be confronted by a host of defending players. This system also allows for considerable mobility and flexibility on both sides of the ball as the attacking midfielder can be pushed forward to create more width on the front line, or the entire diamond can be expanded and shrunk as needed, as well as moved back and forth across the pitch.

The problem areas for defending with a diamond midfield are typically on the flanks as the midfield group often cannot count on assistance from a recovering front-line player. If the tucked-in midfielder steps out to the flank, she can create space inside of her for the other team to exploit if the remainder of the diamond does not move with her. This movement, in turn, may create a strong ball-side defensive presence but dramatically reduce the group's ability to deal with a sudden central or back-side attack if the opponent is able to change fields quickly.

The other spot that can be irksome for a diamond defense is the center of that diamond. As with triangle and box configurations, an opponent in possession in that space can momentarily unbalance the group as it is not clear which midfielder should close down on this player. If no player responds, this player has numerous options to move the ball, particularly wide, and open up the midfield. On the other hand, if two or more players move to pressure the attacker, the diamond can collapse, creating even more room to attack along the edges of the midfield, in particular. In most diamond midfield teams, the players in the diamond have considerable mobility, and the coach must have a high level of confidence in the wide backs to help close down the big spaces in the wide areas.

As with all systems, there are numerous variations of the diamond configuration, and the team can best deal with the threats by rehearsing the likely moves by attackers and the team's intended response.

DEFENDING IN THE MIDFIELD: FOUR PLAYERS, BOX CONFIGURATION: AREAS OF CONCERN

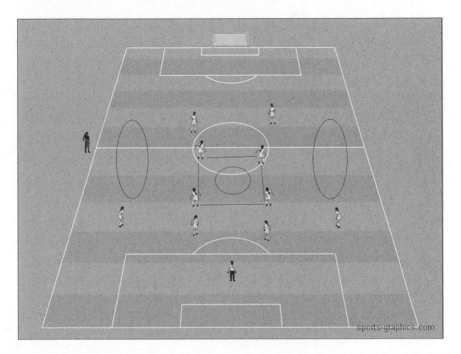

Similar to the diamond arrangement, the box midfield creates a strong, central presence, and concerns on the flanks, as well as a potential danger spot at the center of the box. The added benefit of the box is the assigning of two holding or defensive midfielders, which can provide more protection to the critical space in front of the center backs, in particular, and the provision for two attacking midfielders who can work in support of pressing activities by the forward pair.

As with the diamond setup, the coach will want to be sure the members of the box can cover a lot of ground to help deal with threats and also that the wide defenders are outstanding players who can attack and defend in isolation when necessary.

DEFENDING IN THE MIDFIELD: FIVE PLAYERS: AREAS OF CONCERN

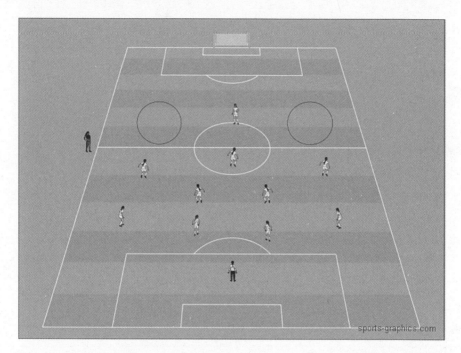

With the blurring of lines and systems in recent years, whether a team considers themselves to be displaying a 1-4-5-1 or a 1-4-2-3-1, or a 1-4-3-3 for that matter, is open for debate. The crucial factor, in this case, of course, is the role of the wingers. Some teams will call these players high wingers in the attack and then wide midfielders when the ball is lost, switching from a 1-4-3-3 to a 1-4-5-1.

For the purposes of this study, it is useful to talk about the advantages and disadvantages of playing a *five-person midfield* on the defensive side of the ball. As the diagram shows, the benefit of defending with five across the midfield is that the coverage of the critical space is much more complete. The team will have two players (the wide back and the wide midfielder) in the outside channels to thwart opponent attacks on the flanks while also keeping a strong block of three in the central corridor.

What the team gains in coverage in the midfield, it loses along the front line. Unless the team play a 1-3-5-2, which is not a common occurrence today, leaving a single front-runner up top will inevitably result in conceding much of the front half of the field to the opponent in possession. Opponents will be able to knock the ball around at their leisure along their back line. For this reason, the five-person midfield is an approach often adopted by teams that expect to face stronger opponents and want to keep the game close, or by teams playing with a lead. Another potential reason is that the team is filled with midfielders and the coach feels the five players will be able to dominate possession. Most often, a team deploying five players in the midfield have another formation in their repertoire (i.e., a 1-4-3-3, simply pushing the wide players to a higher position) that they can switch to in possession or when they need a goal.

DEFENDING ALONG THE BACK LINE: CONSISTENCY AND COORDINATION

Along with the other lines within the team, the back line has evolved considerably in its shape and role over the past generation. Whereas World Cup squads were deploying sweepers behind three- and four-player marking backs with the heavy emphasis on simply destroying play in front of them in the 1980s, virtually all teams now play four (occasionally three) backs in a zonal, "flat" grouping, relying heavily on the goalkeeper and the defenders' organization and mobility to control space and opponents, as well as provide a precise and consistent base for building and maintaining possession when the team has the ball. The increased frequency and complexity of pressing schemes in recent years has been a clear response to this effort to use the back line as a safe area to build attacks. The answer to all of the increased pressure, it seems clear, has been a stubborn insistence that defending players become ever more technical and mobile, able to deal with intense pressure, and also cover much more ground on both sides of the ball to keep the desired shape. Finally, these players have had to become more adept at rapid transition between attack and defense.

MODERN BACK FOUR IN POSSESSION AND TRANSITION: SPACE AND TIME

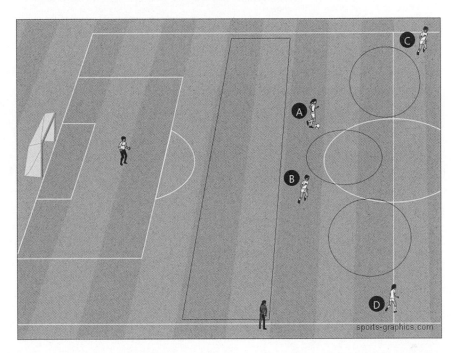

This first diagram highlights the risk/reward associated with modern attacking schemes regarding a standard back four in possession. High-level teams today spread their formations across the pitch when they have the ball, creating a huge shape that allows them to constantly change the point of attack. This constant movement of the ball over distance serves to wear down and stretch a defensive structure, eventually finding openings to attack.

The flip side of this expanded shape is that when the ball is lost, the team, and especially the back line, are in very poor shape from which to defend. The diagram shows center back A in possession nearing the center circle. Her partner, B, is moving away from her, and the wide backs, C and D, have moved to high positions on either flank. Again, this is a great shape from which to be able to move the ball across the field and support the other lines of the team at any angle. When the ball is lost, players must understand the danger for the back line in transition. The spaces between all four backs, and the space in front of the center backs, can serve as outlet zones for an opponent eager to counterattack at speed. Similarly, the space between the back line and the goalkeeper is open to long passes for dangerous attackers wanting to get behind the defenders.

Coaches must spend considerable time emphasizing the importance of getting pressure on the ball immediately upon the loss of possession so that the back line can condense the spaces highlighted in the previous drill. Another aspect of this preparation is the need to train the goalkeeper to support the back line in dealing with the space between her and the backs. Most goalkeepers are reticent about venturing beyond their 18-yard box, but the more space they control beyond the box, the higher the back line can push and the more confidence the group will have in their ability to focus on the space in front of the backs, where most counterattacks are built.

BACK FOUR IN DEFENSIVE TRANSITION AGAINST FACED-UP ATTACKERS IN THE MIDDLE THIRD: DROP AND CLOSE SEAMS

The diagram provides an example of how the expanded shape of the back four behave in transition to defending. The opponents have won the ball in the midfield, and the player in possession has moved ahead of the recovery run of the defensive midfielder. This player has supporting runs as well. Under the circumstances, the back-line players will opt to drop and trade space for time, allowing their wide players (C, D) to sprint back and inside, also in the hope that the defensive midfielder may be able to stop the run of the player on the ball.

BACK FOUR IN DEFENSIVE TRANSITION: WHEN SHOULD A PLAYER STEP FORWARD TO CHALLENGE?

Players along the back line often ask, "When should I step out and challenge an opponent?" While the answer will vary somewhat depending on the experience and qualities of the back-line players, the game situation, and the known qualities of the opponent, there are some basic criteria:

- The remainder of the defending block is properly positioned and can cover the player leaving.

- The attacker is facing away from the goal and can be closed down by the defender before she can turn.

- The attacker is in a position to take a dangerous shot at goal and must be pressured.

- No recovering midfielder can stop the runner.

In the example, center back B has opted to step out and pressure the attacker because the latter has received facing away from goal, appears to have few immediate support options, and the remainder of the back line is in a position to cover her absence and remain numbers-up. It also seems likely that the recovering midfielder will not be able to prevent the attacker from turning by herself, but that she might be able to arrive and double-team the attacker with B.

BACK FOUR DEFENDING: COMMON MISTAKES BY YOUNG DEFENDERS

This is a scenario encountered by many coaches working with young and/or inexperienced players. In the diagram, attacker F is being harried by a recovering midfielder. Attacker E, who is in the seam between the center back (B) and the wide back (D), checks into the space between the back and midfield lines, where she receives a pass from F. D decides to aggressively step into the space in front of B to pressure E. However, in doing so, D has opened up the flank, likely to a direct pass from E to the winger or a lay-off from E to F, who will certainly play into the space vacated by D.

Here are a couple maxims to share with players to help them analyze this situation and avoid opening up the defensive structure:

• In general terms, it's best for back-line players to avoid stepping forward into another defender's vertical zone. Doing so empties a horizontal zone and prevents the player from covering their teammate.

- Although it's important to protect the seam between B and D, it's worth pointing out to D that attacker E is less dangerous in front of an intact back line than the wide player running free behind D when the latter steps inside and forward.

BACK FOUR DEFENDING: DEALING WITH WIDE SPACES IN THE BACK THIRD

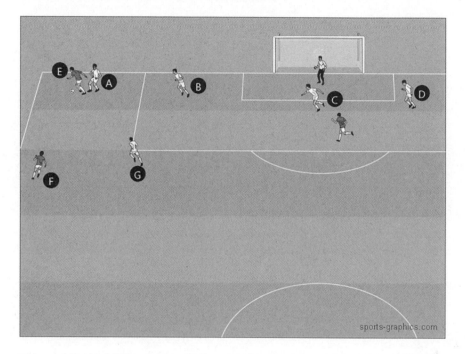

This picture highlights some of the most important components in guiding a back four to deal with threats out wide in the back third. Wide defender A has stopped the forward run of attacker E, turning him away from the goal and driving him toward the touchline, which he can use to further pressure E. Note that A has turned his shin guards up the field, both to defend the end line, as crosses from this space are often the most difficult to defend, and also to try to avoid conceding a corner kick if E tries to bang the ball off E and over the end line. Player B, the center back, is in the process of moving to cover A should the latter be beaten on the dribble. The other center back (C) and the far-side wide back (D) are patrolling spaces in front of the goal should the attackers cross the ball at any point. Note that C and D have turned their bodies to face up-field on arriving, as this posture helps them identify potential targets for crosses and also makes it much easier to play the ball away from the area if a cross is sent in. As supporting attacker F arrives on the scene near the ball, recovering midfielder G moves to ensure the defenders maintain parity in numbers around the ball.

Fabian Holland (right) of Darmstadt forces Carlo Boukhalfa from Regensburg to the touchline, severely limiting the latter's attacking options.
(picture alliance/dpa | Matthias Balk)

BACK-LINE DEFENDING: THREE CENTER BACKS

While the vast majority of teams today play with a four-person back line, there are some teams that deploy three backs. These teams play out of a 1-3-5-2 formation (in the diagram) or, less frequently, a 1-3-4-3. The defensive advantages in either case center around keeping a larger number of players forward, where the front line can pressure the opposing back line or the defending midfield group can congest the space in front of the back line. It's also very easy to create a thick, deep block of players to protect the center of the field on defense. The dangers are also immediately evident. Playing a three-person back line is an invitation for the opponent to try to stretch those players and create bid seams through which to play in the attack. For this reason, teams opting to play three along the back line must ensure that all those players are very mobile, tough individuals, and also players who can communicate and organize well under pressure.

In most modern three-back formations, the players are referred to as *three center backs*, an acknowledgement that their efforts will often be concentrated near the center of the pitch. Most teams will either roll the side midfielders onto the back line in case of a wide threat (creating a four- or five-person back line) or push a holding midfielder down onto the back line in place of a center back who has gone wide to address a threat. Either way, the three-person line quickly shifts to a more familiar, four-person formation.

The need to conduct all this role-swapping is one of the reasons why many teams either do not play a three back, or play some hybrid, for instance, attacking out of a 1-3-5-2 but then shifting in defense to more of a 1-4-4-2.

THE GOALKEEPER'S ROLE IN TEAM DEFENDING

Just as back-line defending has evolved considerably over the past 30 years, the role of the goalkeeper in team defending has also radically expanded. Goalkeepers of the seventies and eighties were often dynamic shot-stoppers with little to contribute to the game on the attacking side unless it was through goal kicks and punts. They also generally had few responsibilities beyond the scope of their own 18-yard box in support of the back line. The back-pass rule (1992) revolutionized the role of the goalkeeper in the team attack, making it necessary for the keeper to be able to receive and distribute the ball under pressure. Similarly, as teams have moved to shrink the space available to an opponent in possession through the consignment of the sweeper to the dustbin of history and the expansion of pressing, the goalkeeper has had to adopt an increasingly ambitious role, effectively controlling the dangerous space behind the defense. Manuel Neuer and others like him epitomized the new generation of aggressive, adventurous goalkeepers who aimed to prevent goals as much through preventing opponent chances as by direct saves. Finally, it's noteworthy that while the best goalkeepers have always been vocal leaders at the back, the increasing complexity of the game has demanded that keepers also provide key reads (i.e., coordinating the control of the space behind the defense) that were often more the purview of the sweepers and other field players in past generations.

BACK-PASS TO GOALKEEPER IN SUPPORT OF BACK LINE

At first blush, this appears to be an attacking, rather than defending, topic. However, the genesis of this situation is a ball in space behind the back line that cannot be retrieved by the goalkeeper (B). Center back A will be able to get to the ball, but he is under heavy pressure from an opponent, and none of the back-line players are in a position underneath the ball to receive a support pass. A, therefore, opts to pass back to the goalkeeper, relieving the pressure. Note that in this case, the goalkeeper has signaled his preference that the ball be played back, not at the goal, but to the side and away from the oncoming attackers. Many youth teams will require players passing back to the goalkeeper to play wide of the net to avoid an errant pass or poor touch by the goalkeeper that would lead to a goal. The longer, angled pass away from the goal will also give the goalkeeper more time to settle the ball and then pass to the recovering wide defender (C). This situation needs to be rehearsed extensively to ensure that the goalkeeper and back-line players can efficiently take away this threat.

GOALKEEPER CLEARANCE ON BALL BEHIND BACK LINE

In this situation, the opponent has placed a ball behind the back line and in front of the 18-yard box. Once again, the center back A is under heavy pressure. This time the goalkeeper (B) sprints from his area and clears the ball. Note that center back A must continue his run toward the ball, shielding the goalkeeper from the attacker's approach. The other center back (D) sprints behind the goalkeeper to cover the goal area in the keeper's absence. The most critical aspects of the goalkeeper's clearance effort are:

- Communicate intentions early and follow through.

- Arrive first.

- Approach at an angle that will allow the ball to be struck without deflecting off an opponent.

- Use the appropriate number of touches (here, just one).

- The ball should be sent high, wide, and far, reducing the risk of it being sent back in before the goalkeeper can return to his area.

- Immediate recovery run.

These situations require frequent rehearsal to ensure sharp decision making and smooth communication between the goalkeeper and the back-line players. The coach can devise a simple exercise with start lines wherein balls can be served in behind or through the back line for the goalkeeper and the defenders to sort out. It's important to serve balls from different angles and distances and some that bounce for the players to practice seeing realistic repetition.

GOALKEEPER AND DEFENDER DEALING WITH POTENTIAL BREAK-AWAY

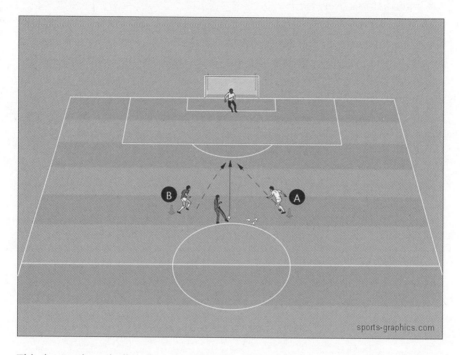

This is another challenging situation for back-line players and the goalkeeper. The coach passes the ball between the runs of the attacker (B) and the center back (A). The goalkeeper cannot be certain that the center back will win the ball or be able to stop B's run to goal.

If the goalkeeper becomes certain the defender will win the ball, he should stay nearer his line and let the duel play out. If the goalkeeper feels that the defender may have a chance to stop the attacker's run, he should allow the defender as much time as possible (usually somewhere near the top of the 18-yard box) before deciding whether to intervene. Cues that the goalkeeper can monitor include the relative speed of the two players and the position of the shoulders of the two players. If the defender can get his shoulder in front of the attacker's (in other words, closer to the goal), then he has a very good chance to win the duel.

If the goalkeeper becomes certain that the attacker will win the race, or if it remains unclear and the two players are approaching the 18-yard box, the goalkeeper will likely need to intervene. Goalkeepers are taught to close rapidly with the attacker and try to block or smother the ball before the attacker can get close to the goal, where the goalkeeper will have difficulty protecting the goal. The recovering defender must pressure B, try to drive him to a bad angle, and also disturb his dribbling or shooting to the point that B cannot finish. If the goalkeeper does intervene, A must continue his run past the goalkeeper to try to clean up any rebound or, if necessary, block a subsequent shot. Again, these situations need to be rehearsed to help goalkeepers and defenders understand each another's tendencies and timing.

GOALKEEPER AND BACK-LINE DEFENDING CROSSES

Crossing situations pose a difficult challenge for goalkeepers and back lines, as the arrival of several attackers, along with the ball, immediately in front of the goal can easily confuse markers and intimidate the goalkeeper. As with other situations involving the back line and the goalkeeper, early and correct reads and sharp communication are critical to defending crosses.

In the diagram, attacker A has beaten wide defender B to the end line and he sends a cross toward the near post. The nearside center back, C, was moving toward a covering position in case A managed to dribble past B, and thus C is played out by the cross. The other center back, D, has tracked a runner to the near post and he is goal side, facing up-field, and ready to challenge the attacker for the ball. Similarly, far-side wide back E and recovering midfielder G have identified dangerous runners and are working to stay or get goal side in case the ball gets past D. Thus, the essential points of emphasis for defenders in front of the goal in crossing situations are to identify and mark the most dangerous runners (those nearest the goal), and in the process of marking, try to face up-field, remain goal side, and disrupt (without fouling) the runner's approach to the goal. This last point deserves special emphasis. Even a bump to an attacker will often cause an errant and less powerful effort at goal by any attacker.

The goalkeeper has numerous responsibilities in crossing situations. First, he must protect the goal from any shot by the player on the ball. As the crosser in this situation is in a very wide, advanced position, there is almost no angle to shoot, so the goalkeeper adopts a position near the middle of the goal, allowing him to cover both posts well if the ball is served near the goal.

Note also the open stance of the goalkeeper. This is a critical, often overlooked aspect of goalkeeper preparation for dealing with crosses. The open stance serves two purposes. First, this posture has the goalkeeper in a better position to observe the action in front of him before the cross is hit. How many attackers approach and from what angles? How many defenders are present to deal with the threat? The goalkeeper must know this information before the ball is sent in, as it affects his calculations as to whether he will attempt to deal with the cross himself or ask his teammates to clear the danger while he remains near his line. The other purpose of the open stance is that it saves vital time if the goalkeeper decides to field the cross. By adopting the open stance, the goalkeeper has saved a step, which may be the difference in beating an attacker to the ball.

The goalkeeper must be trained to make an early, decisive call regarding his intentions. Typically, his call is either "Keeper!" if he intends to go after the ball, or "Away!" if he wants the defenders to deal with the serve. Defenders must listen for and react to the call of the goalkeeper. If the goalkeeper intends to stay near his line, the defender(s) nearest the arrival point of the serve must either increase their contact with the nearest attacker and battle to clear the cross, or perhaps break off contact with the attacker to get to the ball first. Regardless, the defenders' collective goal is to clear the ball with one touch, and if the goalkeeper comes for the ball, then protect the goalkeeper's route to the ball, clear any rebound, and also protect the goal area in the keeper's absence.

TACTICAL GROUP DEFENDING: PRESSING AND COUNTER-PRESSING

The most impactful tactical trend on the defending side of the ball over the past decade has been the increasing popularity and complexity of pressing. More recently, counter-pressing has become widespread as teams focus on transitional moments.

Pressing, broadly speaking, is a team-wide effort to limit the opponent's options in possession and ultimately win the ball. Pressing is typically organized around a series of "cues" or "triggers," which spring the press. For instance, when a team's holding midfielder receives the ball facing his own goal, the action triggers the opponent's press. Built around the team's and opponent's characteristics and the game situation, a press is a coordinated series of actions and movements that must be thoroughly trained for the team to execute together under pressure.

Counter-pressing is a form of pressing, but is, by definition, more chaotic because it is focused on the first few seconds that an opponent is in possession and is keyed more by the presence of team members than any coordinated series of movements. In other words, when the team loses the ball, the nearest players will do their utmost for a limited time or number of passes to win back the ball. As such, fitness and mentality are crucial factors in the ability of a team to counter-press, particularly as the game wears on.

Pressing and counter-pressing are therefore related and complimentary but require careful consideration by the coach to determine the best application of each element for their particular team. The exercises in this section are designed to help the coach build and refine a team press/counter-press.

INDIVIDUAL PRESSING

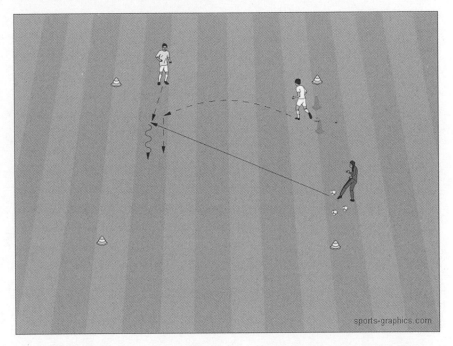

The coach serves a ball to the attacker. The defender starts from the goal he defends and closes down the attacker, trying to drive him away from the goal, as shown. Note that the defender bends his run to guide the attacker to a sharper attack angle and then stays goal side of the attacker. The defender cannot tackle but must use his body and sharp footwork to try to force the attacker to slow his attack or dribble out of the grid. If the defender can delay the attacker for 5 seconds, he wins the duel.

The prohibition of tackling forces the defender to appreciate the importance of body position and manipulating the attacker, as well as patience where needed.

PAIRS PRESSING (1)

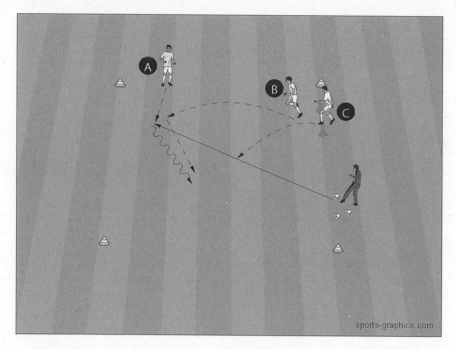

This progression of the individual pressing exercise adds a second defender. The coach serves to the attacker (A), who tries to dribble through the cone goal. The first defender (B) closes down the attacker, interposing himself between the attacker and the goal and trying to drive the attacker to a less dangerous angle. The second defender (C) adopts a covering position, further discouraging the attacker from driving toward the goal. The defenders cannot tackle but win the duel if the attacker stays in the grid for more than 5 seconds or if he is driven from the grid. Encourage proper angles and depth from the second defender, as well as communication, as he should be coaching the first defender to continue to force the ball to sharper angles and those covered by his position behind.

PAIRS PRESSING (2)

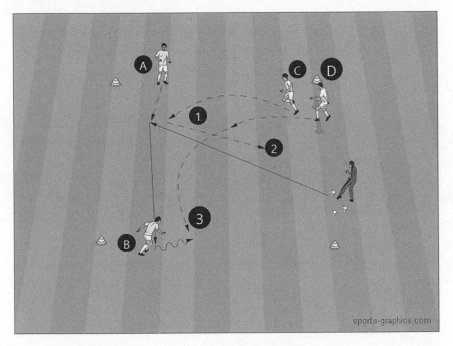

In this progression, a second attacker (B) is added. The coach serves to the attacker (A), who passes to B. The two attackers try to dribble through the cone goal. In this example, defender C moves to close down A and then drops to a covering position when the ball is passed to B. Note defender D's run (3), which is angled to separate B from his partner A, simplifying the defending for the pair. As with the previous exercises, the defenders cannot tackle but can win the duel if the contest lasts for more than 5 seconds or if the defenders can drive the attacker in possession from the grid.

4V4 PRESSING TO FOUR GOALS

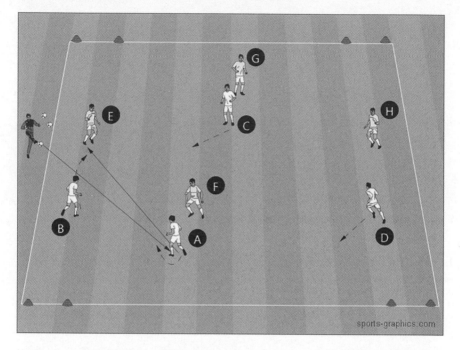

Each team defends two goals along their own end line of the grid. Players try to pass the ball through either of their opponents' two goals. All restarts come from the coach at the side of the grid. In the diagram, the coach passes in to player A, who then turns over the ball to any player on the other team (in this case, player E). This simulated turnover is the trigger for the defending team to press. The corner goals give the players orientation for their pressing. Accordingly, player B moves to pressure E, forcing him toward the center of the playing area, away from the corner goal, and also toward his teammates (C, A, D), who move to positions in support of the defending structure. The coach can use the environment to build collective habits for pressing, showing the importance of manipulating their shape to encourage the attackers to play in central, less dangerous space, and always looking for an errant touch or pass to try to win possession.

4V5 + GOALKEEPER PRESSING

This is a base functional pressing game, allowing front-line and attacking midfield players to explore pressing responsibilities and options. It's important to say at the outset that the coach must adjust the numbers, position on the field, and pressing priorities (i.e., where to direct the ball) based on the needs of the team. In this case, the team is set up in a three-front with a single high attacking midfielder, and they are playing against a standard back four with one holding midfielder and a goalkeeper. The coach has decided to look at pressing options in the front third.

The action is initiated by the goalkeeper (A), who has an extra ball supply. In this case, the coach has dictated that the goalkeeper will not be pressed. The goalkeeper cannot score, nor can the two center backs dribble or score, which is a nod to the fact that most center backs do not pose dribbling threats on match day. The attackers can score in any of the three small goals, while the defenders—if they win the ball—have 5 seconds to score to ensure that the focus here is the pressing.

Coaching topics:

- What triggers the press? Perhaps it's the short distribution by the goalkeeper or a touch by the outside back (B).

- What should the center forward (G) do to support the press? He's outnumbered 3–1, and he has a broad space to try to control. Many youth players struggle with this dilemma, and become frustrated with time. It's important to emphasize that the center forward can have a strong influence on play by getting in between the center backs (D, E) and also by working with the wide forwards (H, I) to ensure that the center backs are unable to pass the ball into space behind the wide forwards for the wide backs to run onto. Further, if the center forward is able to get on a loose ball in the area, he is likely to get an outstanding look at goal with the team in possession spread across the pitch.

- Another important topic in this setting is the importance of the holding midfielder (F) to the attackers' ability to break pressure. Frequently, this player checks into space to receive from any player on the back line and then knocks it to another back-line player, particularly out wide to start an attack. The attacking midfielder (J) should learn to shadow this player and look to deny the ball to him wherever possible. Another interesting topic is the role of the center forward (G) in doubling down on this player in possession if they find themselves nearby.

DESIGNING A TEAM PRESS

When coaches decide to implement pressing options for their teams, there are numerous considerations to ponder. Here is a checklist of terms and variables to consider.

- How often will the team press? Sometimes this will depend on the opponent, but most often, it will be dictated by the makeup and formation of the team that is pressing. For instance, highly fit, mobile teams that play three players across their front line will often press frequently and high up the field. On the other hand, if the team is not particularly fit and only plays a single striker, the team will not be able to press very often, particularly in advanced areas of the field.

- The mentality of the players. Highly driven players tend to thrive in a pressing environment. However, one or two players who simply lack the ambition on the defensive side of the ball to regularly participate in aggressive defending can destroy the team's ability to effectively press and cause internal dissension as the other players sense the lack of effort by their teammates.

- Weather conditions and location. Teams that play in cool weather environments can press more frequently than those in warm weather areas. Altitude is a similar factor, as players unaccustomed to playing in thinner air will struggle to press as the match carries on. It may be more advantageous to press on a wet or bumpy pitch, forcing more errors by the opponent.

- Match situation. Some coaches like to emphasize pressing early in a match to keep their opponents from developing any rhythm in possession. Others will reserve their pressing for later in the match to try and preserving their players' energies for crucial moments. For instance, it is necessary to press late in the match if the team is trailing and cannot wait in a low block to win the ball back after it is lost.

- Where to press? Statistically, there are rewards for winning the ball further up the field, and it stands to reason that winning the ball closer to the opponent's goal will create an advantage on the attack. However, pressing further up the field also carries a much heavier physical load as the space to defend is more expansive, and relatedly, as the team pushes forward, the space behind the defense increases in size too, making the team more vulnerable to passes and runs in behind.

1. *Line of confrontation.* This is the point at which the team will begin to try to win back the ball if the other team is building out in possession. This line can be adjusted depending on the opponent, the match situation, conditions, etc., but designating this point helps the team act in concert to win back the ball.

2. *Restraining line.* This is the level set for the back line when the team is actively defending up the field. Most teams will push near the midfield stripe when the ball is deep in the opponent's end of the field, but teams drop off differently depending on factors including the nature of the back-line players (with quicker players, a higher line can be adopted), the nature of the opponent (faster opponents may dictate that the line drop off earlier and deeper to keep play in front), match situation (trailing late may dictate a higher line), conditions (playing into a heavy wind may dictate dropping off faster), the abilities and proclivities of the goalkeeper (those hovering near their line will not be able to support their defenders and deny space behind the back line), and, critically, the philosophy of team, as teams that want to defend aggressively and further up the pitch will often try to play a higher back line to shrink the space they need to cover.

• Where to force the ball? Part of planning a press is to establish where the team would like to guide the opponent in possession. Much of this decision is dictated by the system of play of the pressing team. For instance, teams playing a three-person midfield will typically try to funnel the ball to a central position along their front line to compel the opponent to play through the area where the midfielders will be concentrated. There are exceptions, however. Some teams will try to use the touchlines as an added defensive pressure source, forcing the opponent to edge in the hope of creating a more predictable pass forward. Another interesting twist on this idea, seen largely at professional level, is the idea that pressing to the touchline will create more stoppages and thus shorten the game. The visiting teams sometimes adopt this posture, greatly disrupting the flow of the game and hoping to limit the home supporters' interest in the match.

- Triggers. When to press is a critical consideration influenced by many of the variables above, from fitness levels to the quality and nature of the opponent, as well as match situation, etc. It is very important to have recognizable cues that the team can use to initiate and execute the press together. For instance, some teams like to press any time the opponent plays a negative pass in their defending half, pushing the opponent further from goal. Another common trigger is to press when the opposing defensive center midfielder receives facing his/her own goal. Whatever the cue, the team must collectively recognize and rehearse the response to be able to respond effectively in the run of the game. Another form of trigger is in the behavior of the players. For instance, some teams leave it to their front-line players to decide when to press. If one player decides to press, the others must follow. On the other hand, if the front-line players tire, they can adopt a lower line and stay with the defending block until they recover a bit or see a good opportunity to press.

A SAMPLE PRESS

The following section gives an overview of how one might design a team press.

SPINE FOR TEAM A

Team A, in the diagram, plays a 1-4-3-3 formation. In addition, the team has the following characteristics:

*   The team plays an inverted triangle in the midfield (two attacking midfielders, one holding midfielder).

*   The team plays in a high-level youth league where unlimited substitutions are allowed.

*   The team coach is experienced and inclined toward an aggressive tactical approach on both sides of the ball.

- Mentally, the players are highly-disciplined and motivated, wanting to earn results to see the team earn a post-season position.

- The team is very fit overall and also deep, allowing them to use a number of quality players along their front line, particularly over the course of a match.

- The team is more athletic than technical, often loses possession, and has to defend.

- The team's back line features a very tall center back, and his partner is the fastest player on the field.

- The goalkeeper is comfortable on the ball and also playing far from his line.

- The team play most of their matches on turf fields also marked for American football, averaging just 65 yards in width.

- The team's season is confined to the fall months, with temperatures averaging 50°F at kick-off. Rain and moderate-to-strong winds are common at game time.

- The team's opponents tend to play indirectly, wanting possession, and building slowly from the back.

- Team A, conversely, plays a wide open style, with much direct play and counterattacking when the ball is won.

TEAM A PRESS DESIGN BASICS

In this diagram, note the *line of confrontation* (A) and the *restraining line* (B). The line of confrontation is the point at which the team will begin to resist the opponent's efforts to move the ball forward. It's important to emphasize that this line is flexible; that is that the coach can move the line forward or back depending on a host of factors, including the match conditions, the opponent, and the relative fatigue level of the team. This line represents an ideal, in the sense that there will be times (i.e., if the press is triggered, or if the team opts to counter-press after losing the ball, or if the team is not prepared to defend at this point and must reform closer to their own goal) when the line will not apply as the team opts to defend higher or lower. Finally, it must be pointed out that if the opponent can push through the zone for defending, as outlined in the diagram, the team will need to drop deeper to defend. In other words, failure at the ideal line does not mean the team will defend any less stoutly; rather, it requires the team to have a plan for how to defend if the effort at the line of confrontation does not result in regaining possession. Team A has adopted an aggressive line of confrontation based on the team's athletic nature and, in particular, the depth at the front-line positions, which will require those players to expend much energy pressing the ball.

The restraining line is the point on the field where the team wishes to deploy the back line to limit the opponent's ability to run and play in behind. In combination with the line of confrontation, use of this ideal allows the team to coordinate its defending efforts. The two lines, as the diagram shows, create a vertically-compressed zone where the team can concentrate to defend.

Like the line of confrontation, the restraining line will vary based on a host of factors, including the team's makeup, the match conditions, and the qualities and tendencies of the particular opponent. This line can vary from match to match or within the run of the game, depending on the team's needs. It also must be pointed out that if the restraining line is punctured by an opponent's attack, the team must continue to defend and must also be prepared to drop to a deeper position in an organized way to reset the defending position.

Team A has chosen a very high restraining line because their goalkeeper can cover the area in behind and is comfortable off his line and playing with his feet. The fact that they have a very fast center back who can run down balls in behind is another factor. Finally, the team is counting on their front line to apply heavy pressure to their opponents and force inaccurate long passes forward, thwarting efforts to time balls in behind.

TEAM A PRESS BASICS: WHERE TO FUNNEL THE BALL

In the diagram, the left winger and the center forward are combining to press the ball to central space, trying to force the opponent to play ahead into the midfield. This is a frequent tendency among teams deploying a 1-4-3-3 formation, as channeling the ball to the center of the field forces the opponent to play the ball to the area where the midfield triangle is concentrated. In the defensive third, the team will push the ball to the edge, where possible, to force the opponent to bad angles near the goal. Note that the triangle has shifted to the left in the midfield area to focus in the funnel being built by the front line. A useful guide is to coach players in the midfield and on the back line to position themselves off the shoulder of the player in front of them, thereby giving some visual focus from which the players can move. Team A has opted to guide the opponent toward central areas because of their formation choice and also because they are an athletic, disciplined group that will be able to sustain pressure over the course of the match.

TEAM A PRESS BASICS: FORCING THE BALL TO THE TOUCHLINE

The diagram shows an important exception to the team's efforts to force its opponent to play forward in the center channel. If the ball is in the opponent's possession within 5 yards of the touchline on either side of the field, the team will use the boundary as an added limiting factor and force the ball to the edge of the pitch. As player A pressures the ball wide, as shown, the midfield and back-line players, in particular left back B, can react by tightening their shape to the line, knowing that player A's pressure will force a pass forward in the narrow channel.

TEAM A PRESS BASICS: "SAFETY" PLAYER

Many teams, particularly those that are aggressive in their pressing, will designate a so-called "safety player." This player, typically a defensive midfielder (A) (see diagram), is required to adopt a more conservative approach, staying home while the remaining front five players press. The idea here is that this designation allows the other midfielders to defend with more freedom, knowing that the safety player will be in place to help disrupt any counterattack that defeats the team's pressing efforts. The safety player also allows the back line to remain intact more often, as they do not need to venture forward to deal with passes into the area in front of the center backs.

Team A has designated player A as their "safety" player because the remaining players in the front six are very athletic, aggressive types that want to chase the ball on defense. Also, because many of the team's opponents prefer to build out of the back, this player will be available to cut out longer efforts to counterattack. (The opponent will likely not be as sharp in their efforts to play directly, given their proclivity to play indirectly, and if the press is successful, the team will win more balls more easily by forcing these errant balls forward). Note that the players may be able to transfer the safety player responsibilities as needed during the match, as fatigue and other circumstances require.

TEAM A PRESS BASICS: TRIGGER 1

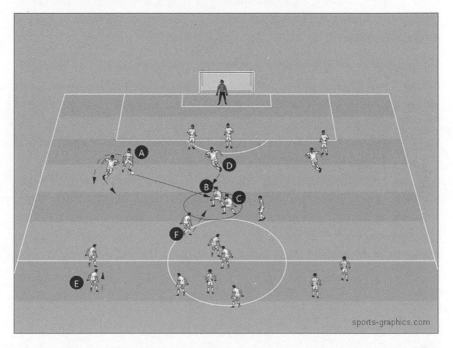

When the basic parameters regarding the team's pressing tactics have been defined, it is then time to assign "triggers" for the team's press. Triggers are situations on the field that present the best opportunities for the team to win the ball because of the tactical situation or the player on the ball. The trigger, in this case, is the opponent's holding midfielder (B) receiving a pass while facing his own goal. The right back (A) has passed into the feet of the holding midfielder, whose options, if he is not allowed to turn, are limited to his back-line support or the goalkeeper. Accordingly, Team A's attacking midfielder (C) recognizes the situation and immediately closes down B, keeping him facing his own goal. He also tries to force the player back in the direction of the pass, making it hard for the man on the ball to open up to the far side of the field, where his options are likely better. Team A's front-line players, particularly the left forward and the center forward (D), try to cut out the passing lanes to both center backs and the player who just passed the ball (A), who is likely to try to move to a higher position to receive a return pass. The center forward's positioning and movement are particularly critical. If the opponent's center backs are split, the work of the attacking midfielder is very important as he needs to guide the player on the ball away from one of the center backs, making it easier for the center forward to cut out the remaining option. In some situations, the center forward can also join in the pressure on the ball, coming underneath to join the midfielders while cutting out support options.

The nearside holding midfielder (F) looks for an opportunity—if the player on the ball is compelled to focus on protecting the ball—to join in winning the ball. Finally, the left back for Team A (E) can tighten up on the opponent's right forward, anticipating the possibility of a pass in this area if the man on the ball is able to turn. It's important that players understand that the press will not always work as the team may not have all of the defending pieces in the right place, or the opponent may find a way to defeat the pressure. However, the pressure may have other positive effects. For instance, by pressuring sharply when the opponent plays into the holding midfielder, the team may make the opponent less likely to play that pass as the match proceeds, instead choosing to play more directly and thus degrading their attack.

TEAM A PRESS BASICS: TRIGGER 2

The team will also use pressing tactics when the opposing right back (A) receives an outlet pass from the goalkeeper. The left forward (B) will step inside and force the man on the ball to the edge of the field. To help influence the ball carrier in that direction, the center forward (C) moves to a higher position, making it more difficult for the right back to play to the goalkeeper or nearside center back. Team A's attacking midfielder (D) has an important role as well. If player A turns back under pressure, facing his own goal, D will push ahead, getting pressure on the nearside center back and allowing the center forward to move higher and cut out a pass to the goalkeeper. If, however, B's pressure forces A to the touchline and facing up-field, then D will cover the closest opponent midfielder, forcing A to play a long, predictable ball toward his team's right forward, who will be tightly marked by Team A's left back. This is a common tactic that works well against teams whose outside backs are not comfortable on the ball and/or that want to build up out of the back.

TEAM A PRESS BASICS: TRIGGER 3

The third and final trigger used by Team A will be any negative pass by the opponent from Team A's defensive third into the middle third. In this example, the opponent's right forward (A) passes back to the right back (B). Team A reacts immediately, with the goalkeeper and the back line all moving sharply forward. This movement leaves the entire opponent back line in an offside position. It is important to note that Team A's left forward must move to pressure player B, as shown, forcing B to either dribble or play another backward or short pass. Without pressure, B may be able to catch Team A's back line moving forward and put a well-timed pass over their heads into dangerous space with his front line still onside.

As the team moves forward, there are a number of important decisions to be made. For instance, the attacking midfielder and the center forward will adopt positions based on the actions of player B. If that player has time in possession, they will both remain closer to their own goals, thickening the defending block and recognizing that, if they move forward too early, they may open up passing space in behind them. If B is under pressure and/or chooses to play backward, then C and D can be more aggressive, charging forward to apply pressure to the holding midfielders and center backs and allowing Team A to clear their lines and defend further up the field. In this sense, it's important to remind the team that this particular trigger may not result in an immediate turnover, but it's still very important for the entire team to move together every time because the pressing action pushes the entire attacking team further away from Team A's goal. Indeed, failure to push out in this situation is frequently a sign that a team is fatigued and/or losing discipline in the match.

1V2 COUNTER-PRESS

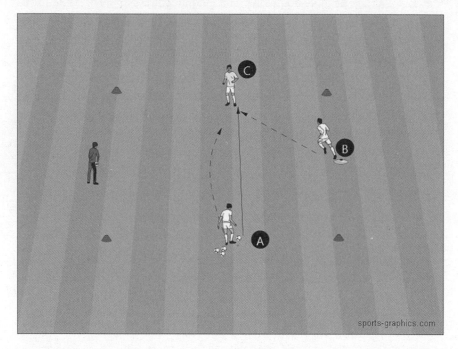

sports-graphics.com

This is a good way to demonstrate to players the root differences between pressing and counter-pressing. Player A passes to player C, effectively turning over the ball to the opponent. Player B is the closest defender, and he moves to close down C immediately when possession is lost. He is less concerned with controlling C's options—though he should work to get C's eyes down on the ball and limit his passing ideas—and more concerned with trying to immediately force a turnover to win back the ball for his team. Echoing this intent, A also joins the pressure effort immediately, bending run to control passing options but also intently focused on getting tight to B and C and forcing the latter to make a mistake. Talk with players about the differences between this approach and the more standard pressing posture. This is an example of a more urgent, improvised effort.

3V3 COUNTER-PRESS

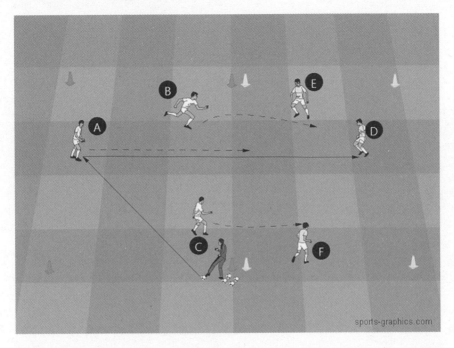

This exercise allows players to experience the moment of the loss of possession and work to win back the ball immediately. The coach passes to player A, who passes to opponent D to initiate the counter-pressing moment. A, B, and C sprint to the grid—where D, E, and F are now in possession—and try to win the ball. Emphasize to the defenders the importance of separating the man in possession from supporting players. In this case, C and B bend their runs to cut out passes to F and E, and then C and B work with A to close down on D, who must be put under heavy pressure and left without options.

If A, B, and C win the ball, they try to keep it and return to their half of the grid. Roles have now reversed, and D, E, and F move to counter-press. Indeed, they should try to win the ball even before A, B, or C can leave their zone. Any ball leaving the area is followed by an immediate restart from the coach, with the player receiving the ball turning it over first time to an opponent. This is an intense, demanding game and should only be played for short 3- to 5-minute intervals.

5V5 COUNTER-PRESS TO END-LINE TARGETS

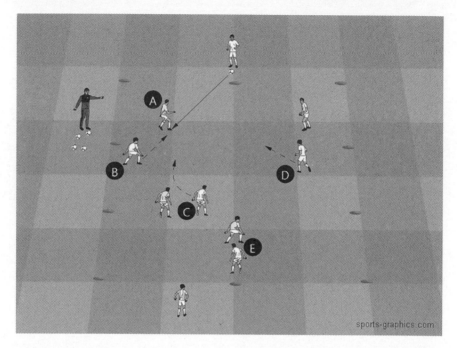

In this exercise, a long, narrow grid makes it easier for the four active defenders to counter-press. Teams play 4v4 on the field, with one player as a target beyond the end line. Play is thus directional, as each team tries to pass to their target for a point. Conversely, teams receive the ball from their opponent after a goal, as shown. The coach restarts play by passing to either end-line target player. This restart simulates a turnover, triggering the counter-press. In the example, defender B moves to press A, who has just received the restart. Player A may not pass back to the target who played him. Players C, D, and E must move to close the space available to the attackers, and if they see that B will get pressure, they must move to assist. It's important to point out the risk/reward relationship here with counter-pressing. If E just barrels forward to assist B, he may leave open a pass to the opponent closest to him or a through pass to the target. What he must do, then, is note that if B can get A facing away and get his head down (so that he cannot assess his options), then C, D, and E can take more risks in joining the pressure.

The directional element is important here as it reminds players that even in a desperate counter-pressing situation, there are still considerations that must be made to ensure that there is a better chance of success for the defenders.

Rotate the target player every 2 minutes.

8V8 COUNTER-PRESSING GAME

This environment allows the team to train counter-pressing in an increasingly functional setting. The two teams play a goalkeeper, three defenders, three midfielders, and two forwards to full-sized goals on half field. It's useful to eliminate corner kicks to keep the game moving; thus, any ball over the end line leads to an immediate goal kick. Similarly, a goal kick follows a goal as well. Otherwise, begin play with no other restrictions.

After a few minutes in which the players settle in and the game develops some flow, call in the team and explain that all turnovers in the run of play now lead to immediate counter-pressing by the team losing the ball. This change will create a much more demanding, intense game. It will also tire the players much more quickly. Therefore, play two 5-minute matches with a short recovery period in between.

Another way to challenge players is for the coach to initiate the turnover sequence. In the diagram, defender A, with the ball, hears the coach holler, "turnover!" and he thus passes the ball to the nearest opponent midfielder (B).

When the team loses the ball, C, B, and D immediately move to pressure B, while A and F, back-line players, move to tighten their coverage of the nearest opponents. The random nature of coach calls for turnovers will force the teams to think carefully about their shape, even when in possession, knowing that they may need to switch to high-pressure defending at any moment.

Another potential teaching point in this environment is the selective use of counter-pressing. Like the pressing scheme laid out in the previous section, counter-pressing can be applied or withheld, depending on the situation. For instance, if the team clears the ball from near their end line to the opponent's defending third, the team will move forward, but it will not be possible to counter-press immediately as the team will be stretched out. Similarly, if the team lead by four goals with 10 minutes remaining, it may not be necessary to counter-press all over the field; it would make sense to save players' energies a bit and employ a more conservative defending style. All these situations can be discussed in this training match, helping players better understand the requirements and employment of counter-pressing.

11V11 COUNTER-PRESSING TRAINING MATCH

This exercise simply takes the counter-pressing measures trained in the previous environments to the full pitch. By playing a training match with full teams, the coach can help the team rehearse crucial aspects of counter-pressing and observe and correct behaviors across units within the team and across the group of 11.

Common questions:

- Do the various groups (i.e., midfielders or the front line) within the team react in coordination to the need to press?

- How is the connection between the lines (i.e., between the midfielders and the back line) as the team counter-presses? It is often this space, if poorly coordinated, that allows opponents to defeat counter-pressing with an outlet pass.

- How long should the team sustain the counter-press? Most teams put a limit on the length of time (i.e., 15 seconds) or the number of passes (often 2–3), and then the team switches to a less aggressive mode of defending. This distinction limits the impact of fatigue, and players should also understand that the counter-pressing moment helps the team by allowing those off the ball to get to better defending positions while also keeping the opponent on the ball occupied so that they find it more difficult to identify longer, more dangerous passes at the start of their attack.

- How fit is the team? Does the ability to counter-press fade over time? This is a common concern, and the coach can use this opportunity to emphasize the importance of fitness and to identify certain "moments" in which the team will counter-press, say the first 10 minutes of each half or after a goal is scored or perhaps only when the opposing wide backs win possession.

TACTICAL GROUP DEFENDING: DELAYED HIGH PRESSURE

Twenty years ago, teams called this posture of defending "low pressure." Concerned that their players interpreted this term to designate less effort and intensity, the term has gradually been modified to "delayed high pressure," emphasizing that this is not a passive defensive stance but rather a conscious decision to apply high pressure at a point closer to the defending team's goal.

Why employ delayed high pressure? There are numerous reasons why this can be a useful approach:

- The area to defend is smaller, allowing for more concentration of the defending team.

- If the opponent is a superior team, defending closer to one's own goal may give the defenders a better opportunity to coordinate their defending, leading to more success. This approach may also slow the pace of the game at moments, which may help the weaker team keep pace.

- If the opponent has demonstrated a consistent ability to defeat pressing and counter-pressing, this approach may give the defenders a better chance to win the ball.

- This approach can conserve energy as the team is defending a smaller space.

- If the defending team has a lead and wants to slow down the game, delayed high pressure may encourage the opponent to play indirectly, building out of the back, which drains more time from the game clock.

- If the defending team lacks ball-winning characteristics as a group, this can be a means of increasing their effectiveness by coordinating their efforts and condensing the space to be defended.

11V11 DELAYED HIGH PRESSURE

As the diagram indicates, the white team is practicing dropping behind the midfield stripe where the group will wait, allowing the attacking team to have possession in their own half but compelling them to attack the massed defending team compressed and waiting for them to come forward.

It's important to emphasize to players that there is overlap in the ideas and terms that comprise defending postures and plans. Teams playing delayed high pressure are setting *lines of confrontation and restraint* closer to their own goal and subsequently *pressing* when the ball reaches a certain point (i.e., the center line) and/or is played to a certain player(s) at or near a given point. In other words, there are *triggers* to be defined and rehearsed to unleash delayed high pressure. Again, the crucial identifier here is the idea that, in this case, there will be high pressure, but the team will be condensing first to try to force the opponent to play into the teeth of a prepared, condensed defense.

TACTICAL GROUP DEFENDING: MID AND LOW BLOCK

The idea of a defending "block" is a long-established component of team defending in soccer. Retreating to a given point on the field allows the defending team to condense space and therefore make it more difficult for the opponent to attack. In today's game, the use of a mid block, in particular, has become very popular both as a means to concentrate the team's defending efforts and also to invite the attacking opponent to spread their energies all over the field, as attacking teams do, thereby creating more space for the defenders to counterattack when the ball is won.

TEAM DEFENDING FROM A MID BLOCK

As the diagram indicates, this team is deploying a mid-block defending concept. In this case, the team have set a line of confrontation at the attacking end of the center circle and a restraining line roughly 10 yards beyond their 18-yard box. It is useful to briefly put players in their shape in this space and talk about the implications, dangers, and opportunities in their positioning. The concentration will certainly make it more difficult to play through the team, though their tight shape comes at a price, as the opponent will not be under pressure in most cases when they have the ball behind the line of confrontation and can use this space to consolidate and organize their attack.

In the case of a mid block, the coach must also decide the team's posture while defending. Is the use of the block primarily to strengthen the defending group's ability to win the ball in the space occupied by the block, and often, therefore, more conservative in mentality, or is the block there to act as a springboard for a high-pressure press? Or is it both, depending on the circumstances? Regardless, the team must know its individual and collective responsibilities and be unified in its intent.

DEFENDING FROM A LOW BLOCK

sports-graphics.com

Here, the team demonstrate a low-block posture. As the diagram indicates, this is a very conservative defensive posture. The idea here is typically that the team is facing a superior opponent and is willing to concede much of the field when the ball is lost to the opponent so the defenders can concentrate near their goal in the hope of defending well together in the tightened space. Other reasons a team might opt for a low block include fatigue, playing down a player, fear of an opponent with fast front-line players getting in behind, or late in a match when the team is playing with a lead.

Teams playing from a low block typically deploy their back line near the top of their own 18-yard box, with the midfield group just 5–10 yards further up the field. Most teams leave a target player near midfield as an outlet and also just to harass the opponent in that space and, if possible, push the attack to a wider, less dangerous space.

The dangers of playing in a low block include a tendency to become passive, as players feel very limited in their ability to pressure opponents. Additionally, there are numerous attacking options available to the opponents with so much space up the field, from overloading a flank and crossing to longer-range shots if space is opened up in the center channel, etc. It can also be very difficult to transition to attacking from a low block, as the defenders are so compressed around their goal that it's hard to find options to relieve pressure while keeping possession when the ball is won. Finally, because the ball is usually won very close to the defending team's goal, any successful counterattacking has to cover the vast majority of the field before a look at the goal can be earned. Still, this is a frequently adopted tactic allowing teams to frustrate their opponents and destroy the flow of the game.

STRONGHOLD DEFENDING—A TACTICAL REVOLUTION

The era immediately preceding the back-pass rule change (Law 12, Section 2) in 1990 was the last period in which defending dominated soccer at the highest levels. That period, loathed by those wanting aesthetically pleasing, attacking soccer, featured packed defenses and physical play. The intervening three decades have witnessed an evolutionary attacking mindset that has blurred systems of play, ceaselessly sped up the game, and presented defending teams with a bewildering array of attacking concepts from Tiqui-taca to lightning fast counterattacks.

It stands to reason that, as in all battles between opposing forces, each side will eventually design tactics to thwart the actions of the opposition. In the ongoing struggle between attacking and defending ideas, the defending side of the ball needs to recognize that new ideas will be necessary to wrest back control of the game. Indeed, it's about control. In the decade ending at the World Cup in Italy in 1990, defending tactics dominated the game. Since then, the attackers have held sway in one form or another. There is an argument to be made that pressing and counter-pressing have been the responses over the past few years, though many would say that these tactics are designed to avoid defending entirely rather than developing any in-depth, thoughtful defending tactics.

Stronghold defending may be the solution for defensive theorists eager to swing the pendulum back toward the defenders. This concept, roughly defined as a progressive, flexible, and oscillating mix of defending postures designed to allow the defending team to dictate the pace and nature of play, is not without precedent, but at this time, there are no clear examples of this tactical approach at the highest levels.

The idea behind stronghold defending is to urge teams to prepare an in-depth, multi-faceted defending plan that allows the team to be more robust and nimbler in its defending. Another way to think of this idea is to challenge coaches and teams to be as elaborate in their defending preparation as they typically are with their attacking plans.

Many teams will opt to press as part of their defending strategy. They go ahead and set a line of confrontation, a restraining line, and some triggers for their press. That's pretty thorough preparation by some standards, but it leaves the initiative with the attackers, who will learn to adjust to the posture of the defense and then how to circumvent the defending team's preparations. What's more, many teams do not have the depth, fitness, or athleticism to just press their way to success. The real challenge is not just to create a thorough defending posture but to be able to use that defending to dictate the game and seize the initiative.

Think, for example, about the National Football League in the United States. Teams scheme on both sides of the ball. The offense's script plays to combat their opponents' defending schemes. The clash of tactics is part of the mental interest in the game. Often, the defenders enjoy some success early in the game as they anticipate their opponents' offensive play selection. It's interesting that frequently after the halftime break, the offenses often adapt to the defending scheme and find ways to score more points. The point here is that tactics change, and being able to adapt is often the difference between winning and losing, and the attackers, if they know what to expect, will often carry the initiative, particularly late in games. Our game, particularly on the defending side of the ball, needs to develop the ability to be more unpredictable.

How can defending teams do that when possession of the ball would seem a mandatory precondition for dictating the game? The answer is to be able to play defense in completely different postures and to be able to blend those ideas in a way that utterly unbalances the attackers, much as good attacking teams do when they knock the ball around for 5 minutes and suddenly play a 70-yard through ball from touchline to touchline. Teams do change defending tactics within matches (i.e., when they have a lead late or when a player is red-carded), but those changes are often dictated by the match conditions, rather than any elaborate effort to consciously move from one defending scheme to another.

Much of the challenge here will be the need to change the way coaches approach teaching defending. Just as many coaches prefer direct or indirect attacking and tend to imprint those tendencies on their team, very few coaches engage in flexible, in-depth defending planning. Coaches that rely heavily on high-pressure, pressing-oriented defending generally don't like to ponder the utility of a low block or much in between. Though many coaches will be familiar with the variety of defending techniques presented in this book, few will want to compel their teams to be nimble enough to switch from one posture to another at seemingly random moments in the game. Yet this seems to be the best way to reliably disrupt their opponent's attacking rhythm, and it also makes one's team very difficult to scout and scheme against.

How would one best consider implementing a stronghold-style defending scheme? Every team will have different variables, from talent and depth to opponent strength and style, as well as considerations such as typical weather and field conditions. That said, there must be enough variety in the defending to disrupt the opponents' ability to settle into a particular attacking mode. The team must rehearse these varied postures extensively and understand how to shift from one defending concept to the next in a seamless fashion. Whether that is a signal from one of the players or a coach, or a preset time interval (i.e., high press for 5 minutes, then a mid block for 10 minutes, perhaps initiated during a stoppage), the changeover must be well-understood by all 11 players. Perhaps the best system, allowing for adjusting on the fly in a match, would be a series of calls initiated by the coach and relayed throughout the team, like an audible called by the quarterback in an American football game.

It's interesting to think about the permutations of this kind of philosophy. A stronghold defending system might include variants that alter the direction the ball is being channeled by the defending group (toward the center or the touchlines), and even that variable might be adjusted to vary the direction based on the opponent or the desire to disrupt the flow of the game. Similarly, the use of double-teams in certain areas of the field might be a feature of one posture, as might forcing the ball to a particular player (i.e., a wide back) who the team feel they can then pressure to turn over the ball. It's also important to match the choices of defending style to the team's attacking tendencies. Teams that want to counterattack will most often want to counter-press to create more attacking opportunities, whereas teams that want to hold the ball for much of the match and attack in an indirect style will sometimes be more open to sitting back a bit, keeping a lot of players around the ball so that they can transition well to being in possession. Perhaps the thinking will be different, but it needs to fit the talent and design of the team. Another variable, more tricky to implement, might be the temperament of the defending team. The team defends in a crunching, physical style, often paired with an aggressive press but also compatible with a low block, and then switches to a more reserved, energy-conserving style for a few minutes. Certainly, an attacking team's rhythm would be affected by such a change of style. A change of formation, slight or extreme, would be another potential aspect of rotating the defense.

The possibilities are many and wide-ranging. The following checklist, while not exhaustive, gives a range of ideas for the coach to consider when developing a fortress-style defense.

STRONGHOLD DEFENDING: A CHECKLIST

Here are some of the tenets of defending that can be tuned to seize the initiative in the match for the team without the ball:

- Formation. Example: An aggressive 1-3-5-2 becomes a more conservative 1-5-3-2.

- Personnel: In youth soccer, players can often be freely rotated to change the nature of the defending. At the advanced level, perhaps roles or positions can be rotated slightly to confuse attackers and rest key personnel.

- Lines of confrontation. Adopt a conservative line to rest players, then raise the line to increase pressure on an opponent.

- Restraining lines. Use a lower line to limit space behind the defense, then suddenly raise it to shrink the space in front and condense the defending group.

- Channeling the ball away from the touchline to channeling the ball to the edge of the field. Again, the opponent will need to adjust to find successful passing patterns to break the pressure.

- Adjusting the shape of the team to create and encourage the opponent to play into different funnels. For instance, a standard three-front creates two funnels between the center forward and the wide forwards, whereas a two-front creates a moving funnel between the two strikers.

- Press volume. Rotating a high press with delayed high pressure can disrupt an opponent's offensive rhythm.

- Press triggers. From any negative opponent pass, to a ball received by the holding midfielder facing his own goal.

- Safety player. Rotating this player but not his position makes the press less predictable, for instance, from one holding midfielder to the other, or playing without a safety player for a few minutes.

- Counter-press to no counter-press. This change abruptly alters the posture of the team when the ball is lost, again leading the opponents to need to adjust their tactics.

- Setting double-team "traps" for the attackers. For instance, in a 1-4-4-2, the wide midfielder and the wide back can often double-team a wide midfielder. Encouraging the pass to the opponent in that position can provide a sudden tactical problem for the opponent. Similarly, a holding midfielder can turn and help a center back double-team an opposing center forward who tends to be a target.

- Set an opponent screen. Use a player from the midfield line to screen out passing lanes into a key attacking midfielder or center forward for part of the match, then free that screening player up to join a pressing movement.

- Play a mid block, then switch to a low block for a portion of the match. The varying areas in which the defense concentrates present different challenges for the opposition.

- Rotating physical, high-energy defending (whether pressing or sitting in a low block) with more reserved, energy-conserving defending is also a means of disrupting an opponent in possession.

- It sounds counterintuitive, but there may be advantages to adjusting the vertical compactness of the team in certain areas of the field to create problems for the opponent. Most teams want to be very compact in defending, and this is certainly how the team is likely to win the ball. However, much like the funneling concept, there may be times when it will be desirable to tempt an opponent to play into a certain space, depending on the team. For instance, a team that has the ability to knock the ball around in their back third, even against a press, and then likes to suddenly pound the ball over the top of the back line for a fast runner(s) may be confounded to find there is no room to play into because the defending team's back line is sitting deep even though they are pressing high. This is not a tactic a team would want to pursue for very long, but it might allow the defenders to pick off a lot of sloppy, miss-hit passes forward for a few minutes.

- Similarly, the team may want to consider altering its horizontal compactness as well. If there is an opponent that appears unable to play longer balls to switch fields, the defending team may be able to play with a hyper-condensed shape when the ball is on one side of the field, drawing in far-side wingers and wide backs to make the defending block even more dense. Again, this would likely be a temporary tactic, but it would make it very hard to play through the group.

In summary, the idea behind a stronghold-style defending scheme is to find a range of defending postures that suit the team and their defending strengths and then rotate those postures in such a way as to be able to unbalance an opponent in possession and maintain the initiative in the match even when the team does not have possession.

DEFENDING AT SET PIECES

Remarkably few coaches would say, if pressed, that they spend enough time training their teams to execute attacking set pieces, much less defend in these situations. Many coaches treat set pieces as the last topic to address at the end of camp, before the first match. On the defensive side, the practice usually involves a brief discussion and a few walk-throughs of wall-building and defending corner kicks. How many coaches have observed a session on defending set pieces at a coaching clinic? I have not—in 30 years of coaching—because I am confident no one has ever put one on the agenda at an event I attended.

This is a gaping hole in our coaching preparation. Given the outsized influence of set pieces on the outcome of matches, it would seem common sense that a sensible, regular diet of set-piece defending education and rehearsal would be a staple of team training.

The simplest explanation for the ongoing dearth of preparation in this area is that the topics are not any fun to teach and don't fit well into any standard exercise progression. Coaches don't like to disrupt the flow of training to talk about the subtleties of defending short corner kicks or the team's philosophy in defending goal kicks. Indeed, we're all sensitive to the effect this sort of slowdown has on the posture and energy of our players.

How do we help our players understand the importance of defending set pieces to success on match day while keeping their focus and energy at training? The most common answer to this question is that coaches try to spoon-feed defending set pieces to their players, introducing or rehearsing one aspect (i.e., defending long-throw-ins) for 5 minutes in the middle of training as a sort of active rest. If players become accustomed to this presentation, the active rest can be an effective form of training and imprinting set-piece defending principles.

An additional method that is especially effective for rehearsal of set-piece defending involves splicing together a bunch of isolated occurrences from within the game (i.e., defend a long throw, corner kick, direct free kick needing a wall, indirect free kick) into a sequence, as a group of players are confronted with these situations one after another, creating an active and efficient training environment from what had been isolated, static restarts. This type of training is both flexible (include whatever the coach wants to focus on), and dynamic for the players. A pair of examples of this type of training are included near the end of this chapter. However, as the coach opts to address defending set pieces, understanding the many variables and coordinating the team response will be critical to the team's ultimate success.

DEFENDING KICK-OFFS

STANDARD TEAM SHAPE: DEFENDING KICK-OFFS

Every year, highlights are posted of teams shocking their opponents with a goal seconds after a kick-off. It stands to reason that the cause is more often poor preparation by the defending team rather than a brilliant stroke by the attackers. As shown, most teams adopt a condensed, narrow shape when defending kick-offs. The focus is shortening distances between defending players and also posting more players to defend the most direct routes to goal.

While these are important steps, the other crucial element here is psychological. An outsized proportion (as high as 70% in some studies) of goals are scored in what we often call "twilight," which is the first and last 5 minutes of the half and the 5 minutes after a goal. Whether players are slow to get into a start of a match, wear down in the final minutes, or relax after scoring a goal, many of the scenarios precipitating these goals spawn from what seem, at first blush, like innocuous kick-offs. Coaches must prepare their teams for these moments by including and defending kick-offs in training games and making clear the implications of the "twilight" period so that teams can avoid let-downs at key moments.

DEFENDING KICK-OFFS: HIGH PRESSURE

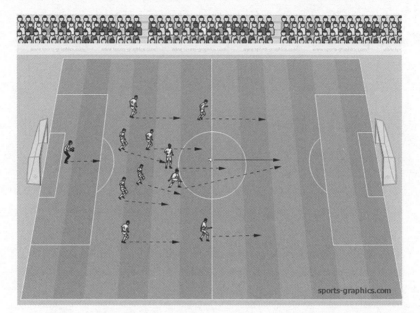

One approach that many coaches use to avoid seeing their teams victimized by a kick-off goal is to react sharply to a back-pass off the kick-off through a high-pressure defending surge. This tactic has the dual benefit of getting players moving (as slow movement often contributes to conceding a goal from a kick-off sequence) and possibly forcing an error by an unsuspecting opponent, which could quickly turn the tables, creating a chance for the team that was defending the kick-off.

The caveat with the forward surge shown in the diagram is that players need to understand that opponents, wary of being caught flat-footed in possession in their own end, will often kick a ball deep into their opponent's end off the kick-off. If the entire defending team is running forward, a very ugly breakthrough could follow for the attackers. It's important, therefore, to condition players to read the intentions of the player in possession. Players about to hit long balls take a long touch, look up and follow with a big back-swing from their kicking leg before clubbing the ball over distance. If this sequence appears imminent, back-line players (and the goalkeeper) in particular must prepare to drop off and deal with the serve. Emphasize to front-line players that if their pressuring runs are immediate, they may be able to interfere with this long serve.

DEFENDING GOAL KICKS: A STANDARD LOOK

Goal kicks present an opportunity for the defending team to force a turnover high up the field and perhaps catch the opponent unprepared to defend critical spaces. In the diagram, the goalkeeper for the defending team adopts a position near the top of his 18-yard box, prepared to run onto a long serve by the opponent and also to receive a back-pass if his teammates have to retreat to win the ball under pressure.

The back line is near the midfield stripe, tightly marking the opponent's front-line players at the top of their formation, particularly on the side of the field where the restart is being prepared. Similarly, the midfield group has shifted to the ball side, and they are in goal side, tight-marking positions with each of the likely midfield targets for the kick. Finally, front-line players have an important role to play in these situations. They should mark potential outlet players along the opponent's back line, but the attackers are usually outnumbered in these situations, and it's important that the forwards work together in response to any short kick or shanked ball by the goalkeeper that might present an opportunity.

DEFENDING GOAL KICKS: TEMPTING THE OPPONENT TO PLAY SHORT

As teams develop defending strategies, many will use cues to initiate their pressing efforts. Among the more common triggers is a pass to an outside back, and many coaches set up their teams to encourage opponents to make the short pass on goal kicks. The key player here is the forward assigned to deal with the outside back after the pass. This player must linger far enough away from the wide back to tempt the goalkeeper to play the ball there, but not so far that the forward will not be able to immediately close down the wide back when he is targeted.

With the recent change in the rules regarding the taking of goal kicks, the player taking the ball can now play short, inside the 18-yard box to a teammate to restart play. This complicates matters somewhat for defenders, as now the center forward may need to rush into the 18-yard box and bend his run to try to force the ball out to the wide back to initiate a pressing sequence. The midfield group may also need to adapt by shading to mark or pressure the other center back, denying the attackers a short, central outlet.

DEFENDING PUNTS: CONCENTRATION AND DEPTH

sports-graphics.com

Although not strictly a set-piece situation, punts are analogous to many restarts, with the start and stop of action and the long distribution. Defending these situations can be very challenging, particularly for young players not accustomed to dealing with the ball in the air. The diagram gives an overview of important principles for defending punts. In general, teams try to concentrate their shape, particularly along the back and midfield lines, as it is very important for the defenders to get the first touch on any punt to deny the attackers a quick touch in behind or the ability to settle the ball and start their movement forward. Another conceptual preference here for youth teams is to get the defensive midfielders to a depth where the ball is expected to arrive. This adjustment will allow the defense to keep more depth, as the center backs can cover in behind the defensive midfielders rather than committing immediately to winning the ball, often by stepping forward.

DEFENDING CORNER KICKS: "MAN" MARKING

Debate rages in the coaching community regarding the best means of defending corner kicks. There are, in essence, three choices. First, some teams rely heavily on what is termed "man" or person-marking. Other teams will mark zones, and most today use a blend of person and zone marking in these dangerous situations.

The advantages of person-marking include the defenders' ability to choose their match-up (i.e., tallest defenders on tallest attackers, etc.), person-markers are inherently active as they are chasing their mark, and all the contact and chaos tends to throw off timing and runs for attackers, making it harder to connect on the serve.

There are also many inherent weaknesses in heavily person-marking in these situations. First, markers can easily be rubbed out in their runs, as collisions and picks are happening with every kick, resulting in a wide open finisher. Second, since the attackers are dictating the flow of movement, they can run everyone to one spot and hope to get an open look away from the ball if a lone attacker gets lost. Finally, and critically, everyone, both attackers and defenders, are running at the goal. Even if the defenders get the first touch, where are they to go with the ball? Sometimes the ball can be flicked out of danger, but in other situations, it's very difficult for defenders to have a useful touch running all out at their own goal. Given these concerns, it is rather surprising that many youth and professional coaches continue to rely upon person-marking schemes to deal with defending corner kicks.

DEFENDING CORNER KICKS: ZONAL SCHEMES

sports-graphics.com

Contrary to person-marking schemes are zonal-based defenses for corner kicks. In these setups, players generally deal with areas of the danger space rather than tracking specific opponents. The advantages of adopting zonal defending at corner kicks include the selection and placement of defenders based on need rather than where the opponent shows up and the maintenance of a clear defending shape, with straightforward clearing duties for every player, as opposed to both marking and clearing duties.

In the diagram, the outside backs are on the posts. The center backs and a holding midfielder are in zones across the top of the 6-yard box, with another, tighter line featuring the other midfielders and one forward in front, and a single forward out wide set to distract and interfere with the server while a lone forward stays near midfield to serve as a focal point for clearances and counterattacks. There are many variations to the shape of zonal defending, and coaches adjust the players' positions to fit their priorities and concerns. A recent trend has been to remove one or both players from the posts, with the idea that they are better used in expanding the zones covered or in person-marking, but this also leaves no cover for a goalkeeper venturing to deal with the serve.

Coaches who shy away from zonal marking systems tend to be annoyed at the inactivity of their players. As players settle into their zones, the argument goes, they tend to get complacent and fail to react to the serve, often getting beat to the ball by an onrushing attacker. Another issue is the fact that, unless the team make special arrangements to deal with them, the opponent's best attacking options—often tall center backs adept at winning the ball in the air—are running free and can steamroll through space occupied by a zone-defending, petite midfielder or back.

DEFENDING CORNER KICKS: ZONE/PERSON-MARKING MIX

The most common theme of corner kick defense in today's game is the blending of zonal and person-marking schemes. In the diagram, the defenders have placed players on each post and set up a zoning group across the 6-yard box, but they have also placed three players in person-marking assignments, picking out the most likely targets for the opponent's serve. Finally, the defenders still have a player near the corner to distract the server and one near the midfield stripe as a target for clearances and counterattacks.

Some teams, particularly late in games when protecting a lead or potential draw, will put all 10 field players in their box, mixing them into the marking/zone scheme. Although this move thickens the traffic in front of the goal and may create a better chance to clear the serve, it's worth noting that it will likely draw more opponents further forward, too, since they do not have to worry as much about a counterattack off the kick. Most teams use a "+1" theory when scheming for attacking corner kicks, meaning they try to keep one more defender near midfield than the number of players left there by the team defending the corner kick.

Paderborn's goalkeeper Jannik Huth (middle) clears near Darmstadt's Thomas Isherwood. (picture alliance/dpa | Bernd Thissen)

DEFENDING CORNER KICKS: DEALING WITH SHORT PLAYS BY THE OPPONENT

Short corner kick plays have long been a subject of coaches debating whether to serve the ball into the area, perhaps try to create an overload out wide or, in the case of Pep Guardiola's Barcelona and Manchester City sides, simply restart possession. Whatever the merits of the various short corner options, our concern here is the defensive implications of opponents sending multiple players to the corner. Some teams send no players to deal with this situation, resolving that their structure hold firm in front of the goal. This is a reactive, arguably dangerous position, as the attackers can close at their leisure to the goal before shooting or serving, with the goalkeeper stuck in a crowd in the area. A more common tactic is to either send one player or station one player along the end line and let that player deal with the attackers. This approach, however, also leaves the defending team subject to an overload situation, where one player may get free and approach the goal area before serving or shooting. Perhaps the ideal approach is to match the number of attackers at the corner by shuttling a person-marker from the group in front of the goal (see diagram) to the corner. Once there, the two defenders sort out who deals with each opponent, and as soon as the ball is put in play, the defenders move to destroy the attack. Often, confronted with equal numbers, the attackers will send one player back inside, which the defenders can match, and change the play. The only concern with this response is the possibility that the defenders prefer the short corner to having a ball launched in front of the goal or that the sending of two players so denudes the defending structure before the goal that the coach opts not to send equal numbers to defend at the corner. Regardless, the team's strategies for dealing with short corner kick situations (including those where the attackers add a second player late, running one from the back line or the group in front of goal) must be thoroughly rehearsed to prevent defending mistakes.

DEFENDING CORNER KICKS: DEALING WITH A PLAYER SCREENING THE GOALKEEPER

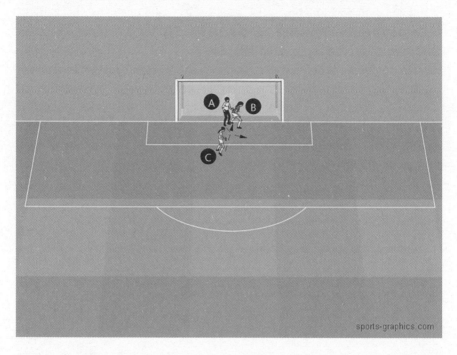

Among the more annoying issues coaches often cite as concerns in defending corner kicks are the problems created by an attacker sent to screen the goalkeeper's movement to the ball. This is first and foremost a rules issue, and there is enough gray area to continue to encourage coaches to distract and even pick the goalkeeper as she moves to deal with the serve.

Paraphrasing the rules, the attacker has the right to be there but not to specifically inhibit the goalkeeper's movement to the ball. This is where the gray area comes into play. In the picture, attacker B has stationed herself in front of goalkeeper A. Although B cannot technically block A's movement to the ball, she can slowly move toward the ball, effectively screening the goalkeeper's movement. While some officials monitor this situation and call it more closely to defend the goalkeeper, others don't see much of a concern here and allow a fair amount of contact and blocking to occur.

One way to confront this issue is to detail a center back (C) or another defender to step in between the goalkeeper and the attacker and deflect the movement of the attacker away from the goalkeeper's approach to the ball. This can be an effective means of freeing the goalkeeper to move, but it also adds another body in the way of her movement, potentially increasing the likelihood of preventing her from getting to the ball. Some goalkeepers, particularly those of imposing physical stature, prefer to deal with the attacker on their own by stepping around the attacker as the ball is being hit. Regardless of how the team choose to deal with this conundrum, the coach should point out politely to the official before the kick that the goalkeeper appears to be marked and request that the official ensures that her movements are not illegally inhibited.

DEFENDING FREE KICKS

Preventing free kick goals involves numerous points of preparation, from playing to avoid conceding free kicks in critical spaces to rehearsing the building and composition of walls and the careful marking of potential targets in non-shooting situations. Unlike corner kicks, for instance, free kicks originate from anywhere on the field, and the coach must ensure that the team understands the variables associated with the different locations and types (indirect or direct) so that on game day, the team knows exactly how to respond.

FREE KICK FROM DISTANCE

sports-graphics.com

When free kicks are conceded in the attacking half and well beyond shooting range, the team will generally try to get all of its players goal side of the ball and then set a holding line (B, above), both to condense the area available to the attackers and also to create an offside space that will ease the job of the goalkeeper to protect the area behind the line. Players along the back line should mark attackers that push into their areas, denying them a clear route toward the goal. Note that the wide attackers also drop behind the ball and pinch in, adding more players to the defending block and tempting the player taking the kick to avoid the most direct routes to goal. Note that the center forward, player A, takes a slow walk past the ball, putting himself in the way of any fast service and buying precious time for his teammates to establish the defending block. Many teams will have this player linger 7 or so yards from the ball, encouraging the opponents to ask the official to move the player to the 10-yard required distance. The presence of the player in the area can be a useful distraction. The front-line players (A, C, D) must also be aware of any effort to play short and fast (i.e., a pass to the right back from the attacking team, which might be followed by a quick pass down the touchline or a serve in behind), as they must be ready to apply enough pressure after the quick restart to discourage dangerous serves forward.

DEFENDING FREE KICKS: SLOWING THE KICK AND SETTING THE DEFENSE (1)

In the moments after a free kick from a dangerous position is called by the official, the defending team must act quickly to delay the kick and buy time to set up their defending structure. In the diagram, the official has just whistled a foul against the white team. Two of the attackers in the area move to place the ball and prepare to take the kick. The nearest defender (A) stands close enough to the ball to block any effort at the goal. While this is technically not legal, the player often uses the pretense of injury, confusion over the call, or arguing with an opponent to stand in the way, and this is essentially standard practice, though it's important to show some level of subtlety and not stand right on top of the ball or kick it away, as a yellow card may be shown.

While one team member slows down the preparations by the attackers, the other field players must move to their positions to defend the kick. Typically, back-line players move to mark the most advanced and dangerous attackers, as well as hold a line that offers some offside protection for the goalkeeper while midfielders fill in the wall (B). Front-line players are also often in larger walls, and they can come closer to the goal if more markers are needed, too. Most teams leave a single forward near the midfield stripe to prepare for a counterattack and compel the opponent to leave at least two players back.

Finally, the action of the goalkeeper (C) in this phase is very important. The goalkeeper must focus immediately on the possibility of a quick shot. Note that her position in this diagram shows her ready to deal with a shot, not adjusting the wall. Attackers will notice if there is a possibility of a quick shot, and if the goalkeeper is standing at the post talking to her teammates, she will likely be unable to deal with an effort at goal. Rather, she must wait in a central position, ready to save, until the opponents request the player and wall being built by the defenders be moved to the appropriate distance (10 yards) from the ball. Once the referee intervenes and says that play will restart with her whistle, the goalkeeper can then move to adjust the wall.

DEFENDING FREE KICKS: SLOWING THE KICK AND SETTING THE DEFENSE (2)

In this diagram, the official has interceded at the request of the attackers to move the wall back. Because the action is stopped until the official's whistle, the goalkeeper (C) now moves to the post to adjust the defensive wall. A useful rule of thumb is to place one player outside the keeper's line of sight to the ball from the post, allowing for some bending of the ball by a skilled shooter. The means of communicating with the wall are an important consideration here. If the goalkeeper simply hollers "left!" and "right!" her directions may not be heard. Professional goalkeepers often kick the aluminum posts to get the attention of their players in the wall. It's important to give visual signals as well. Pointing the direction to be moved (and hollering) and then giving a palms-up stop when the wall is set is essential to good communication. The player on the post side of the wall must look over her outside shoulder or turn to face the goalkeeper to receive these directions, and then the members of the wall have to pull on one another to make sure they move together. Rehearse these details to ensure crisp execution on match day! In area B, note that the defenders have all moved to goal-side position of the attackers in the area, and they work to keep their bodies between the attackers and the goal, with the idea of wrecking the timing of runs to goal and allowing the goalkeeper as much space and time as possible to deal with a shot.

DEFENDING FREE KICKS: SETTING THE DEFENSE (3)

In this diagram, the defense is prepared to confront the free kick. Note the final position of the goalkeeper, as she lines up off the shoulder of the last defender in the wall. From this position, she trusts the wall to deal with any shot to the part of the goal covered by her teammates while she positions herself to see the ball and cover the remainder of the goal. It's important to note that attackers tend to try to either shoot over the wall or try to blast the ball through the wall, and the goalkeeper must be ready to move to cover behind the wall if needed.

DEFENDING FREE KICKS: A TALLER WALL? (4)

This diagram demonstrates the latest in ideas of how to extend the height of the wall and take away the most preferred type of shot from direct kick situations. For years now, coaches have asked their players in the wall to jump a bit to extend the height of the wall. As a result, attackers have resorted to driving balls along the ground, often pushing an effort through the base of the wall and on goal. Recently, teams have started placing a player on the ground, as shown, behind the wall, with the thought that if the wall jumps high, the player lying behind them will block efforts on the ground. This is a bit of a concern from a player safety standpoint (the laying player would do well to at least tuck her head down and forward to avoid taking a shot to the back of her skull), and coaches are advised to think carefully about placing a player in this vulnerable position.

DEFENDING FREE KICKS: ADDING A "BULLET" (5)

Many teams will use what is called a "bullet" to disrupt indirect free kick opportunities in dangerous spaces. In the diagram, the end player in the wall sprints at the ball as soon as one player from the attacking group moves to start their play. This movement may be carded by the official for encroachment, but if the "bullet" times his run to arrive just after the first touch, he's often successful in blocking the shot effort or disrupting the timing of any play involving a setup touch by the attackers.

Referee Felix Zwayer (middle) shows Dortmund's Marco Reus (left) the red card. (picture alliance/dpa | Bernd Thissen)

DEFENDING SET PIECES: EFFICIENT, LIVELY TRAINING

One of the challenges of training defending set pieces is the often-stagnant nature of the session, which is a result of a lot of stopping and starting. Players often lose interest or become mechanical in their actions, and the training tends not to replicate match situation intensity. One solution for this dilemma is to play a training match where every restart results in a dangerous set-piece for one team or the other. For instance, if a team concedes a throw-in, the team must instead defend a corner kick. If the team concedes a corner kick, instead there is a direct free kick from the dangerous space near the 18-yard box. It's important, from a coaching perspective, to be prepared to move the game along quickly, having extra balls on hand and time limits to execute restarts, but this method can create more intensity for the players.

sports-graphics.com

A second means of adding quality to the training of defending set pieces is the use of a series of consecutive set pieces, as highlighted in the diagram. A defending group deals with building walls to defend direct kicks, setting the line and marking to defend an indirect kick, defending a long throw-in and defending a corner kick, all in quick succession. Rotate the groups. In this way, teams get concentrated training in assembling and executing key defending moments around set pieces.

SITUATIONAL DEFENDING

A final consideration in preparing a team to defend is assuring that the group are prepared to adapt to situational challenges that may occur during a match. These situations typically compel a team to adjust their defending shape and/ or priorities based on events, the match score, or the time remaining and may be difficult to address on match day if the team is not properly prepared.

DOWN A PLAYER

Whether there is a red card issued or an injury, teams often find themselves playing short at crucial times in a match. It's important for the coach to replicate these conditions by playing with uneven teams in training and interrupting a training match to remove a player so that the team can adjust as needed.

PLAYING WITH A LEAD (1)

If the team is leading, particularly late in a match, the team may adopt a more conservative defending posture, adding another defender, withdrawing an attacker, etc. Players should be well-versed in slowing down the game, putting the ball out of bounds, committing mild fouls, etc., to make it difficult for an opponent to mount an effort to erase the lead.

PLAYING WITH A LEAD (2)

The player on the ball, whose team has a lead, dribbles the ball toward the attacking corner, compelling the trailing team to chase him down, draining precious final moments from a match. All players must understand this tactic, using the time gained to consolidate their defending block behind the ball.

PLAYING FROM BEHIND

When teams trail late in matches, players are often substituted or moved as the team adopts a more risk-oriented posture to try to erase the deficit. It's common to see a team add an additional front-line player and remove a back-line player to try to apply more pressure to the opponent, and the team often plays more directly as a result. Teams must be well-versed in coping with these changes during the match.

DOWN A GOAL

The team above has added another player to its front line (four attackers) and withdrawn a defender (three defenders), and they are playing more directly. The consequences of this change for the team's defending are important. The back three must understand their expanded role and the fact that the team will be stretched vertically, so they must anticipate having to deal with large spaces to defend. Additionally, the front-line players must be highly motivated to win the ball immediately when it is lost, given that they have more numbers and that the opponents will likely try to play long to drain time from the match.

OPPONENT TACTICAL CHANGES

Another important consideration is the behavior of the opponent. Some teams will drastically alter their formations, personnel, and tactics during the match. These changes, particularly against superior teams, may dictate the need for a team to alter its defending posture to meet the new threats. If the opponent inserts front-line players who possess speed that cannot be matched by the other team's defenders, that team may decide to play a lower restraining line to keep play in front of them or, conversely, to high press to try to disrupt potential service to these players. Another prominent example is the insertion of a tall center forward. This player is likely to be the target of crosses and service in the air, and his or her presence may dictate that the defending for the opponent involves trying to deny service to that player. Most often, the changes spark only minor adjustments, but it's important for the coach and team to be on the same page each match as to how to respond to such changes.

"TWILIGHT"

Statistically speaking, a disproportionate number of goals are scored in the opening 5 minutes, the last 5 minutes of each half, and also in the 5 minutes after a goal is scored. Match-opening nerves, fatigue, the psychological let-down of giving up a goal, or the relaxation inherent in scoring a goal all affect the mental performance of players in the course of the game. As such, coaches must thoroughly prepare for these "twilight" situations where the game can be turned through smart defending. Many teams do their utmost not to allow the ball anywhere near their goal after kick-off, opting to kick the ball deep into their opponents' end with the restart and defend from far in front of their goal. These defending considerations must be drilled into the team in training so that the group can respond through intelligent defending on match day.

REFEREEING

Coaches often lament the inconsistency in officiating throughout matches and across entire seasons. One set of officials may allow very physical, aggressive play, while another may enforce a tidier, finesse-oriented match environment. Either way, teams must adjust their defending behavior to either take advantage of the wide open, aggressive conditions or the need to play more conservatively, as the referees dictate.

WEATHER

Compounding or suddenly changing weather can also influence a team's defending tactics as a match progresses. Wet surfaces may cause an opponent to play more directly, as may gusty winds. Conversely, rising temperatures and humidity may cause a team to want to hold the ball as a form of defending with the ball, trying to avoid chasing the opponent around the pitch to regain possession. Whatever the circumstances, a team must be prepared to alter defending posture and tactics based on weather incidents that influence the match.

Paris Saint-Germain vs. Bayern Munich in the driving rain.
(picture alliance/dpa | Sven Hoppe)

CONCLUSION

In conclusion, this book addresses the critical concepts necessary to build effective individual and team defending skills and tactics. It is also a resource book, offering explanations of dozens of different exercises and variations designed to help the coach keep the teaching of defending varied and interesting. Finally, the author has sought to argue that the onus is on coaches to create varied, rotating, and in-depth defending schemes that allow teams to seize and hold the initiative in every match. Good wishes for your coaching.

BIBLIOGRAPHY AND SUGGESTED READING

Interviews and Conversations

John Pascarella. Head Coach, Oklahoma City Energy (USL).

Jeff Tipping, United Soccer Coaches Director of Coaching Education Emeritus.

Nathan Klonecki. Executive Director, St. Croix Soccer Club.

Print and Field Sessions

Ancelotti, Carlo. *Quiet Leadership: Winning Hearts, Minds and Matches*. Penguin, 2016.

_____. *The Beautiful Games of an Ordinary Genius*. Rizzoli, 2010.

Anderson, Chris, and David Sally. *The Numbers Game: Why Everything You Know About Soccer is Wrong*. Penguin, 2013.

Athanasios, Terzis. *Jürgen Klopp's Defending Tactics*. Soccer Tutor, 2015.

_____. Marcelo Bielsa: *Coaching Build Up Play Against High Pressing Teams*. Soccer Tutor, 2017.

Balague, Guillem. *Pep Guardiola: Another Way of Winning: The Biography.* Orion, 2012.

Bangsbo, Jens. *Fitness Training in Soccer – A Scientific Approach*. Reedswain, 2003.

_____. *Defensive Soccer Tactics*. Human Kinetics, 2002.

Barney, Andy. *Training Soccer Legends*. Soccer Excellence, 2006.

_____. *Coaching Advanced Soccer Players: 40 Training Games and Exercises*. Reedswain, 1999.

Bate, Dick. *The Dick Bate Football Anthology,* 2019.

Bate, Dick, and Ian Jeffreys. *Soccer Speed*. Human Kinetics, 2015.

Beale, Michael. *The Socccer Academy: 100 Defending Practices and Small Sided Games*. Reedswain, 2007.

—————————. *The Soccer Academy: 140 Overload Games and Finishing Practices*. Reedswain, 2007.

—————————. *Training Creative Goalscorers*. World Class Coaching, 2008.

Beswick, Bill. *One Goal: The Mindset of Winning Soccer Teams*. Human Kinetics, 2016.

Bisanz, Gero, and Norbert Vieth. *Success in Soccer Volume 2: Advanced Training*. Phillipka-Sportverlag, 2002.

Blank, Dan. *High Pressure: How to Win Soccer Games by Smothering Your Opponent*. Dan Blank, 2017.

—————————. *Shutout Pizza: Smarter Soccer Defending for Players and Coaches*. Soccer IQ, 2014.

—————————. *Soccer IQ: Volume I*. Dan Blank, 2012.

—————————. *Soccer IQ: Volume 2*. Dan Blank, 2014.

Borbély, Laco, Peter Ganczner, Andi Singer, and Jaroslav Hřebík. *All About Pressing in Soccer*. Meyer & Meyer, 2018.

Calvin, Michael. *Living on the Volcano: The Secrets of Surviving as a Football Manager*. Century, 2015.

—————————. *No Hunger in Paradise: The Players. The Journey. The Dream*. Century, 2017.

Carson, Mike. *The Manager: Inside the Minds of Football's Leaders*. Bloomsbury, 2013.

Cox, Michael. The Mixer: The Story of Premier League Tactics from Route One to False Nines. Harper Collins, 2017.

—————————. *Zonal Marking: From Ajax to Zidane, the Making of Modern Soccer*. Bold Type Books, 2019.

Crothers, Tim. *The Man Watching: A Biography of Anson Dorrance, the Unlikely Architect of the Greatest College Sports Dynasty Ever.* Sports Media Group, 2006.

Cruyff, Johan. *My Turn: A Life of Total Football.* Nation Books, 2016.

DiCicco, Tony and Hacker, Colleen. *Catch Them Being Good.* Penguin, 2002.

Dorrance, Anson. *Training Soccer Champions.* JTC Sports, 1996.

Dost, Harry, Te Poel, Hans-Dieter, and Hyballa, *Peter. Soccer Functional Fitness Training: Strength, Motor Skills, Speed, Endurance.* Meyer & Meyer, 2016.

Dure, Beau. *Long-Range Goals: The Success Story of Major League Soccer.* Potomac Books, 2010.

Englund, Tony. *Goalie Wars! Goalkeeper Training in a Competitive Environment.* World Class Coaching, 2010.

_____. *Players' Roles and Responsibilities in the 4-3-3: Attacking.* World Class Coaching, 2011.

_____. *Players' Roles and Responsibilities in the 4-3-3: Defending.* World Class Coaching, 2011.

_____. *Style and Domination: A Tactical Analysis of FC Barcelona.* World Class Coaching, 2012.

_____. *The Art of the Duel: Elite 1 vs. 1 Training.* Foreword by Anson Dorrance. World Class Coaching, 2014.

_____. *Competitive Small Group Training: Maximizing Player Development in the Small Group Setting.* Foreword by Tony Sanneh. World Class Coaching, 2014.

_____. Complete Soccer Coaching Curriculum for 3-18 Year Old Players Volume I. NSCAA, 2014 (contributor).

_____, John Pascarella. *Soccer Goalkeeper Training: The Comprehensive Guide.* Meyer & Meyer, 2017.

_____, John Pascarella. *Soccer Transition: Moving Between Attack and Defense.* Meyer & Meyer, 2019.

Ferguson, Alex. *Leading: Learning from Life and My Years at Manchester United*. Hachette Books, 2015.

Fieldsend, Daniel. *The European Game: The Secrets of European Football Success*. Arena Sport, 2017.

Franks, Ian, and Mike Hughes. *Soccer Analytics: Successful Coaching Through Match Analysis*. Meyer & Meyer, 2016.

Gordon, Jon, and Mike Smith. *You Win in the Locker Room First: The 7 C's to Build a Winning Team in Business, Sports, and Life*. Wiley, 2015.

Gregg, Lauren. *The Champion Within: Training for Excellence*. JTC Sports, 1999.

Harrison, Wayne. *Soccer Awareness: Developing the Thinking Player*. Reedswain.

————————. *Coaching the 4-2-3-1*. Reedswain, 2011.

————————. *Coaching the Flex 1-3-3-1-3: Adaptable Tactics for the Modern Game*. Reedswain, 2015.

————————. *The Art of Defending, Parts I and II*. Reedswain, 2002.

————————. *Recognizing the Moment to Play*. Reedswain, 2002.

————————. *Game Situation Training for Soccer: Themed Exercises and Small-Sided Games*. Reedswain, 2005.

Honigstein, Raphael. *Das Reboot: How German Soccer Reinvented Itself and Conquered the World*. Nation Books, 2015.

————————. *Bring the Noise: The Jürgen Klopp Story*. Nation Books, 2018.

Hyballa, Peter, and Hans-Dieter Te Poel. *German Passing Drill: More Than 100 Drills from the Pros*. Meyer & Meyer, 2015.

Jankowski, Timo. *Successful German Soccer Tactics: The Best Match Plans for a Winning Team*. Meyer & Meyer Sport, 2015.

Jones, Robyn, and Tom Tranter. *Soccer Strategies: Defensive and Attacking Tactics*. Reedswain, 1999.

Kaspers, Willy. *Precise Passing – Perfect Combination Play*. Institute of Youth Soccer, 2016.

Kouns, Chris. *Counter Attacking in the Modern Game*. World Class Coaching, 2016.

Lloyd, Carli and Coffey, Wayne. *When Nobody was Watching: My Hard-Fought Journey to the Top of the Soccer World*. Houghton Mifflin Harcourt, 2016.

Lucchesi, Massimo. *Pressing*. Reedswain, 2003.

Luxbacher, Joseph A. *Attacking Soccer: Tactics and Drills for High-Scoring Offense*. Human Kinetics, 1999.

Lyttleton, Ben. *Twelve Yards: The Art and Psychology of the Perfect Penalty Kick*. Penguin, 2014.

Neveling, Elmar. *Jürgen Klopp: The Biography*. Ebury Press, 2016.

Perarnau, Martí. *Pep Confidential: The Inside Story of Pep Guardiola's First Season at Bayern Munich*. Arena, 2014.

_____. *Pep Guardiola: The Evolution*. Arena, 2016.

Pascarella, John. Field session, 2016 NSCAA Convention.

_____. Field and Classroom presentations, NSCAA Master Coach Certificate, 2015.

Power, Paul, Hobbs, Jennifer, Ruiz, Hector, Wei, Xinyu, and Lucey, Patrick. *Mythbusting Set-Pieces in Soccer*. 2018 Research Papers Competition Presented by Major League Baseball.

Pulling, Craig. *Long Corner Kicks in the English Premier League: Deliveries into the Goal Area and Critical Area*. Kinesiology, (2015), 47(2):193–201.

Rivoire, Xavier. *Arsene Wenger: The Biography*. Aurum, 2007.

Roscoe, Phil, and Mike Vincent. *Modern Attacking & Goal Scoring*. World Class Coaching, 2010.

Schreiner, Peter. *Tactical Games – Part I*. Institute of Youth Soccer, 2018.

_____. *Tactical Games – Part 2*. Institute of Youth Soccer, 2018.

Seeger, Fabian. *Creative Soccer Training: 350 Smart and Practical Games and Drills to Form Intelligent Players - For Advanced Levels*. Mayer & Mayer, 2017.

Tipping, Jeff. *Drills and Exercises to Develop the Elite American Player.* Jeff Tipping, 2012.

_____. Session presentations at the NSCAA Conventions.

Toplardan, Duran, Gollerin, Atılan, and Analizi, Niceliksel. *Quantitative Analysis of Goals Scored from Set Pieces: Turkey Super League Application.* Journal of Sports Sciences, 2016, 8(2):37–45.

Tsokaktsidis, Michail. *Coaching Transition Play - Full Sessions from the Tactics of Simeone, Guardiola, Klopp, Mourinho & Ranieri.* Soccer Tutor, 2017.

Turek, Steven. *Fundamental Attacking Strategies.* Institute of Youth Soccer, 2016.

Tweedale, Alistair. *The Growing Role of Set-pieces: A Premier League Trend or a brief Aberration on our Beautiful Game?* Telegraph, August 8, 2019.

Verheijen, Raymond. *Conditioning for soccer.* Reedswain, 1998.

Walker, Sam. *The Captain Class: The Hidden Force that creates the World's Greatest Teams.* Random House, 2017.

Wilson, Jonathan. *Inverting the Pyramid: The History of Football Tactics.* Orion Books, 2008.

CREDITS

Cover and interior design: Anja Elsen

Layout: DiTech Publishing Services, www.ditechpubs.com

Cover photo: © AdobeStock

Interior diagrams: © Meyer & Meyer Sport

Managing editor: Elizabeth Evans

Copy editor: Sarah Tomblin, www.sarahtomblinediting.com

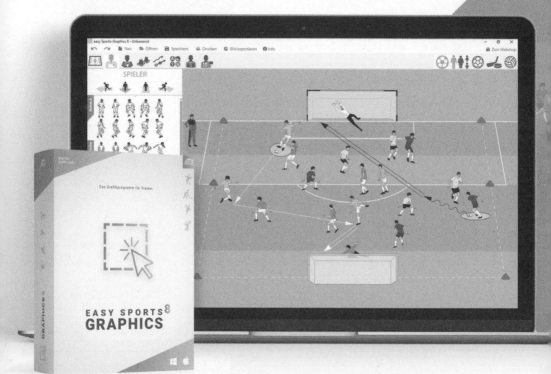

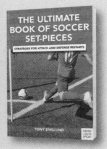